4 Stormy Trials of
Veer Savarkar

4 Stormy Trials of
Veer Savarkar

Alas! None, a fair one...

Harindra Srivastava

Research & Editing
Tej N Dhar

PRABHAT
PRAKASHAN

Published by
PRABHAT PRAKASHAN PVT. LTD.
4/19 Asaf Ali Road,
New Delhi-110 002 (INDIA)
e-mail: prabhatbooks@gmail.com

ISBN 978-93-5266-676-8
4 STORMY TRIALS OF VEER SAVARKAR
by Dr. Harindra Srivastava

Edition
2025

Price
₹ 300.00 (Rupees Three Hundred only)

Printed at
R-Tech Offset Printers, Delhi

Preamble

My first book on Savarkar *Five Stormy Years: Savarkar in London* was published in 1983, the birth centenary year of Savarkar. I hailed it as 'a centenary salute' to my hero, and wrote it after six months of research odyssey in India (visiting all places and meeting all people associated with Savarkar) and some two months' of dust-eating at all prime libraries and research centres of London, Paris and Holland.

The book was published by Allied Publishers and launched at the Dadar residence of the eminent music maestro Shri Sudhir Phadke in the august presence of Shri V. Shanta Ram and Shri Bhalji Pendharkar, the two doyens of Marathi and Hindi Cinema and also close associates of Savarkar. The book was a "dream-product" or a kind of "Command performance." In the midnight of April 20, 1981, Savarkar appeared in my dream to tell me to do some concrete and creative work on one of the facets of his life which had remained unexplored. For instance, his five turbulent years in London and Paris which rocked the entire Europe and whose tremors were felt as far as America. The "Gaelic American" was constantly in touch with him and regularly covered his activities. I woke up with a thud and never looked back till the dream came true. The mission was accomplished in about two years and the book, as planned, was born on May 28, 1983. Several astronomers and astrologers who heard the dream story have called it a clear case of *'parkaya pravesh.'* However, I have kept my lips tight, till today.

No sooner the book was released, in fact, even earlier, previews and book excerpts flooded the media. More than ten national dailies lavishly reproduced regularly some portion of the book. It was followed by 30 to 40 reviews in English, Hindi, Marathi, Gujarati, Punjabi, Bengali and Tamil in newspapers, magazines and journals. The uproarious coverage also earned me three National Awards. This was soon followed by more reviews, readers' reactions,' invitations and felicitations both at home and abroad, such as UK, France, Holland, Switzerland (University of Geneva), Mauritius, Thailand, Belgium and Singapore, where many I.N.A. offiers had carefully preserved the translated copies of Savarkar's book on 1857 distributed to them by Netaji during their oath-taking ceremony. He went on to define it as *The Gita of Indian Soldiers.* As a result, the first edition vanished in less than three years. Even the second edition is still out of print. Besides being translated into Hindi by Rajpal and Sons (1984) and Marathi (1989) by Dhanshree Publishers, Vadodara, it was also translated into Tamil (so I learnt from a letter by Mr. C. Ginamony of Madras), but owing to some mishap it could never see the light of the day. The Hindi translation entitled *Udit Martand Savarkar London Mein* has already undergone three reprints and is also out of print. Since then, I have done eight more books in English and Hindi on various aspects of this protean genius. But as Tennyson's Ulysses says, "Yet all experience is like an arch where through gleams the untravelled world whose margin fades as on and on we move."

Savarkar is an ocean, infinite and fathomless. And we are mere Newtons gathering puny pabbles on the shore. To some extent, this book can be taken as a sequal to my first book and surely the last "the swan's song," as they say. As a chronic patient of "Savarkaritis," I have loved and lived him......... lived with him, so to say. For this I have also paid an exorbitant price for more than four decades, such as rejection of registration for a Ph.D. by Delhi University (which later, I did from Nagpur), rejection of a T.V. serial shot in Europe at my own cost. (the reason given was that it might breed violence and terrorism among youths) and withholding my D.Litt Degree for last 18 years by Shivaji University of Kolhapur. And last, but not the least, rejecting and returning my Hindi biography of Savarkar by National Book Trust soon after 2004 election results. The irony being that the book was not submitted by me for publication, but was assigned to me by the then Chairman of the Trust, Shri Brij Mohan Sharma. All this reminds me of Savarkar's prophetic warning to one of his admirers who, during a historic press conference at Hotel Janpath on 12th May, 1957 had asked. "Since your health is fast deteriorating ...... what is your advice to the younger generation." Savarkar replied with a cryptic smile "Well, youngman, love me if you like but don't follow me blindly..... for that will cost you dearly as you have already seen my turbulent life." He quoted a Sanskrit Shloka which says, "I am a Blazing Sun, I do give Heat, Light and Life. But dare not come too close to me. Thou shalt simply singe thy wings...."

And yes! I have singed my wings but I have no regrets. For I have succeeded in excavating him from the dark dungeons of deliberate vendetta, marginalization, and humiliation. After all, how long can one shield the blazing Sun. The eclipse is over and the world is increasingly rediscovering his latent dimensions. In UK and Europe alone, where once his writings were banned, at least four researchers have earned their doctoral degrees with my assistance and guidance. There are many more in the pipeline. As a seer and visionary that he was, most of Savarkar's warnings and prophesies are emerging on the national horizon and will soon be *'THE TRUTH OF TODAY.'*

Just one example --

Some two years before his *atma-arpan* (willing surrender of his soul to the super soul) when Savarkar was convalescing, a group of senior journalists led by Vidya

Dhar Gokhle, MP (who narrated it to the author) during his daylong visit with his family at his Gurgaon residence) visited Savarkar Sadan on May 28, 1964. Congratulating him on his 81st Birthday he asked only one question, "Tatya Rao, when will this ungrateful country realize and recognize your sufferings, and contribution in liberating the motherland." Faintly smiling, Savarkar shot back, "Tell me, Vidyadhar, how many centuries it took to discover the divine magnificence of Ajanta and Ellora frescoes? In my case, give me only half a century and see what happens"? Came 28th of May, 2014..... the day Savarkar had asked for. At 11 a.m., the Prime Minister Narendra Modi garlanded the portrait of Savarkar in the Central Hall of Parliament. Overwhelmed with ecstasy, he could barely murmur, "Savarkar Ji ... your day has come at last."

The obvious implication being that some day all your national dreams and forecasts shall also come true. The Eternal court of Eternity is yet to give its verdict.

And sooner, than later ....

—Harindra Srivastava

Introduction

Our book is an account of the trials that Vinayak Damodar Savarkar, popularly known as Veer Savarkar, faced in England and Holland, in the first decade of the twentieth century, because he passionately strove to work for the freedom of his country from the British yoke, and the trial that he had to face in post-independence India, along with many other people, for Mahatma Gandhi's murder, in 1948.

Right from the time of his schooldays, Savarkar was awash with supreme devotion for his country. It is unbelievable that as a young boy in his early teens he should have been pained by his country's sad plight with the intensity that we associate with the pain of mothers for their afflicted children. For him, the country was truly his motherland, which he treated with the reverence that one has for one's mother. We emphasize this, because this kind of devotion is hardly appreciated these days. In fact, in the changed cultural climate of our times, "motherland," "nationalism," and "patriotism" are no longer lauded, and are invoked by people, almost grudgingly, only when our soldiers and security forces lose their lives while fighting our enemies.

The intention behind providing this account is not merely to give details about how unfairly Savarkar was treated in all these trials, first at the hands of the British and then at the hands of the newly formed government of India, the heroic manner in which he faced them, and the sufferings that they brought in their wake for him and his family and friends, but also to lay the basis for a much more important consideration: a sorely needed historiographic intervention.

This intervention needs to be put in its proper context so that its legitimacy is understood, as it should be, in its proper spirit. We hardly need to labour the point that is too well-known by now: that recreations of the past, which take the form of historical writings, acquire a distinctive shape and character because of the person(s) who undertake to write them. Savarkar himself made us aware of this when he wrote his well-researched account of the happenings of 1857, which he looked at differently from what had been the general trend till then. While the imperial historians, and even some Indians historians who accepted their version uncritically, characterized the fight of the Indians against the British as an uprising, the Mutiny as it was known for a long while, Savarkar called it India's war of independence, and his fight against the British as its continuation.

We invoke this detail to help the readers understand that almost all the major accounts of freedom movement in India have focussed largely on what we think is only its later and less important part, in which leaders like Gandhi and Jawaharlal Nehru figure prominently. We believe that viewing the freedom movement from this restricted perspective leaves out a crucial part of this account, in fact, the very start of what was actually a freedom struggle, when a group of dedicated revolutionaries staked their lives to take this fight into the very backyard of the British, to give sound blows to its dominance by shaking its very foundations, whose reverberations were felt and heard all over the world. This was the time when both Gandhi and Nehru, though older than Savarkar, were not even visible on the political horizon.

Because of this limited way of looking at the narrative

of India's freedom, the contribution of the person central to our book, and also his daring associates, has been denied his rightful place in this narrative, which he so richly deserves. Another thing that we need to stress here is that our contention about the true nature of this narrative is not merely our opinion but a truth that has been acknowledged and commented upon by the very powers that oppressed us for more than two centuries and granted us freedom in 1947.

For this, we refer to the meeting that Justice B L Chakroverty, the Chief Justice of India, had with Lord Atlee in Calcutta, in 1947. This is what he writes: "When I was acting Governor, Lord Atlee, who had given us independence by withdrawing the British rule from India, spent two days in the Governor's palace at Calcutta, during his tour of India. At that time, I had a prolonged discussion with him regarding the real factors that led the British to quit India. My direct question to him was that since Gandhi's 'Quit India Movement' had tapered off some time ago, and in 1947 no such compelling situation had arisen that would necessitate a hasty British departure, why did they have to leave? In his reply Atlee cited several reasons, the prominent among them being the erosion of loyalty to the British crown among the Indian Army and Navy personnel, a result of the military activities of Netaji. Towards the end of our discussions, I asked Atlee the extent of Gandhi's influence upon the British decision to quit India. Hearing the question Atlee's lips became twisted in a sarcastic smile, as he slowly cleared out the word 'Mi-ni-mal.'"

Since this statement about the immediate cause of India's independence from the British comes from no less a person than Prime Minister Atlee, it carries weight and compels us to rethink on the narratives of freedom that give too much importance to the contribution of Gandhi and Nehru.

A close look at Atlee's observation brings out two interrelated facts. One, that the British decision to quit India was least influenced by the movement led by Gandhi. And two, that the British were compelled to quit the country because they perceived that their control over it had weakened, because of the activities of Netaji.

If Netaji's activities and their effect on the Indian Army and Navy is of crucial importance in India's freedom struggle, then it becomes necessary to see what led Netaji to do what he did. Our contention is that the base for a violent opposition to the British rule in India was laid by Savarkar, right from the time of his school-going days, as will be clear from the account that figures in Chapter 1. For now, we would only like to mention that the erosion of loyalty in the Armed Forces was the direct result of the activities and writings of Savarkar at a time when both Gandhi and Nehru were busy indulging themselves in the very place where he had challenged the British might. But first about the Bose-Savarkar connection.

When Bose qualified the ICS in England, he decided not to join the Indian Civil Service, because joining it would have meant colluding with the British to oppress the people of his country. Savarkar too did not want to serve the British after completing his education. In fact, this was the condition on which he had accepted the scholarship to study Law in London. Because the British government had been warned by the intelligence agencies in India that they needed to keep a watch on Savarkar, that "born firebrand," they held him guilty of indulging in anti-British activities, and, among other things, blocked his rightfully earned legal degree.

Bose called on Savarkar in Bombay in "Savarkar Sadan" on June 22, 1941, after his differences with the Congress Party had reached a point of no return, and Gandhi had made sure that he quit the office of the President of the Party. In that meeting, Savarkar told him not to waste his time on activities that could only land him in prison. He advised him to smuggle himself out of the country and try to reach Germany and Japan and raise an army of liberation from the thousands of Indian prisoners of war. By accepting his advice, Bose virtually carried out Savarkar's plan of violent struggle against the British.

Another interesting thing to note is that when Bose visited the Andamans on December 30, 1943, as the supreme commander of the *Fauj*, he paid his tribute to the people who had fought the British and were imprisoned in the notorious jail there. He arranged for the printing of the Tamil version of the *Indian War of Independence of 1857* and distributed it among the soldiers as their Gita that they needed to treasure.

In his speech from Cathay Pacific on Azad Hind Radio, Singapore, on June 25, 1944, Bose gave credit to Savarkar for thinking ahead of his times by emphasizing the importance of military training for the country's youth: "When due to misguided political whims and lack of vision, almost all the leaders of the Congress Party have been decrying all the soldiers in Indian Army as mercenaries, it is heartening to know that Veer Savarkar is fearlessly exhorting the youths of India to enlist in armed forces. These enlisted youths themselves provide us with trained men and soldiers for our Indian National Army."

In short, the point we are trying to make is that if the British felt threatened by Bose's activities and the loss of loyalty among the Indian Army, the basis for this was created by Savarkar's actions and thinking, which Bose has openly acknowledged. Savarkar too paid tribute to him during the celebrations associated with the dissolution of *Abhinava Bharat* in 1952.

To understand the achievement of Savarkar in its proper perspective, it is important to know how Gandhi and Nehru lived as students in London and what they thought about the British around the time he was dealing violent blows to the British by organizing protest marches and meetings, inspiring a large group of dedicated young men to play with their lives for attacking the symbols of British power, and running a vigorous propaganda campaign against their unjust ways in virtually all the countries of Europe. This makes us see how effective Savarkar was at that time, and why it is unfair not to give him his rightful place in the narrative of India's freedom.

Let us first look at Gandhi. When he went to study in London, in 1880s, he behaved like an aristocrat. Dr Sachedananda, who too was in London around the time, says that he cannot forget the way Gandhi looked when he met him for the first time, because he wore clothes that were the very acme of fashion, and believed "more in fashion and frivolities than in acquisition of knowledge," and was a "swell" and a "masher."

The description given by Sachedananda is well worth quoting: "Gandhi was wearing a high silk top hat brushed 'burnish bright,' a stiff and starched collar (known at that time as the Gladstone), a flashy tie displaying all the colours of the rainbow, under which there was a fine striped shirt.

"Gandhi wore a morning coat, a double-breasted vest, dark striped trousers to match, patent leather boots, and spats! He carried leather gloves, and a silver-mounted stick."

The contrast between the style of Savarkar, who lived a spartan life in London in India House, busy studying and also doing everything possible to rally support for the freedom of his country, and that of Gandhi is quite striking.

When Gandhi visited London in 1909, during the time he stayed in South Africa, he met Savarkar in India House. He was invited by its inmates to preside at a dinner function organized on the occasion of *Dussehra,* which fell on October 24. After hearing Savarkar's speech, Gandhi admitted that it was one of the finest speeches he had listened to in many years.

The ideological divide between the two surfaced openly when Gandhi reacted to the assassination of Curzon Wylie by Madanlal Dhingra on July 1, 1909. He happened to be in London at that time as part of the Indian delegation from South Africa. And his response, which was absolutely uncalled for, was couched in a language that one cannot normally associate with a person who swears by non-violence. He mourned the loss of Wylie, and called the act of Dhingra "childish and cowardly." He also attacked Savarkar, indirectly, when he said: "In my view, he [Dhingra] has acted like a coward. He was egged on to do this act by ill-digested reading of worthless writings." The writings, which he considered worthless, are an oblique reference to the writings of Savarkar, which were meant to instil in young people a fiery desire to destroy the English presence in India. These included his books on Mazzini and the heroes of the war of independence of 1857.

More abusive language flowed from Gandhi in response to the statement that Dhingra made in the court in his defense. Though praised by the very people against whom it was directed, political leaders like Lloyd George and Winston Churchill, who compared Dhingra with "Plutarch's immortal heroes," Gandhi had only contempt for what he had said and spoke about it very disparagingly: "His defence of himself, too, appears to have been learnt by rote. The statement, according to me, argues mere childishness or mental derangement."

Gandhi obviously wanted to project himself as a pacifist and it so happened that much later, when he moved to India and took control of the Indian National Congress, a vast multitude of common Indians accepted him for what he advocated. Many leaders of the party who did the same accepted his dictates obediently, and if anybody chose to differ with him, Gandhi made it difficult for him to stay in the organization. We have already stated what he did to Bose, who was compelled to leave the Congress Party only because Gandhi saw to it that he was not allowed to function as the lawfully elected President of the Party.

Because of Gandhi's authoritarianism and aggressive individualism, many discerning observers of the Indian struggle have stated things about him that many admirers of Gandhi may not like. Guy A Aldred, for example, goes to the extent of saying that by siding with Wylie, Gandhi showed that "he was the enemy of the Indian struggle. He was not a pacifist. He was not a saint. He was a politician and, as such, responsible for the partition of India, and for the terrible atrocities that followed upon that partition." Aldred derides his pacifism as a pose, which many people in the West accepted only because of their ignorance. He says that he was not: "I recall his support of the Zulu war, his support of the First World War, and his support of the Second. A weird pacifist, this! The part he played in the independence negotiations, his attitude towards partition, his close association with the Mountbattens need not be detailed.... From Gandhi's love of dictatorship, from his desire to be the Mahatma, Pakistan was born."

We have deliberately avoided to dilate on the two most loathsome episodes of the Mahatma's saintly life: his demonic encroachment upon poor Kasturba on the day his father died and his relationship with his friend Hermann Kallenback in South Africa.

Gandhi himself admits that he was a failed Mahatma, in his letter to Mahadev Desai, written on September 15, 1919: "... all my vows of *Tapasya* (self-restraint) and *Brahmcharya* (celibacy), which were extolled to the skies, were utter failures; ... one who started sex gratification with his wife at an age of 15 and continued to indulge in it fairly often for 30 years, what praise does such a one's *Brahmcharya* met? It is just like that cat which, after having killed several hundred mice, decides to give on a pilgrimage to Mecca" (in Hindi: *nau sau chuhe kha ke bili Haj ko chalee*).

And now about Nehru, the blue-eyed boy of Gandhi. He was in London around the time Savarkar was giving a hard time to the British and making the world aware of the atrocities that they were committing against the Indians. Nehru had been told expressly by his father not to go near India House. His biographers have written about his stay there and come up with interesting details about his lifestyle and his adventures and misadventures and his extravagant habits that put off his father no end. Even his sympathetic biographer Sarvepalli Gopal tells us that in London, Nehru was, "very much the gay man of fashion—'very well-dressed, well-mannered, almost European.' Music concerts, golf at Crowborough, tennis at the Queen's Club, watching cricket at the Lord's and waltzing on ice-rinks, rather than attending lectures at the L.S.E. and devilling at the law, took up his time...[he] found himself often in debt, was forced to pawn his watch and chain, sometimes had no money even for bus or tube fare, and more and more frequently approached his father for supplementary grants."

Gopal also writes that in 1911, Nehru spent around £800, which "in those years enabled most Indian students to pay for a stay of three years in London." This so much alarmed his father that he was compelled to write sarcastic notes to him. Gopal also mentions how on a holiday in Norway, he was saved from being engulfed by a swirling current by a friend, about whom Stanley Wolpert says that he could have been the person with whom he had homosexual relations, for he had pronounced leaning of that kind.

Thus, we see that while Gandhi and Nehru were in London, they had no time or inclination to do anything for their country and hardly showed any understanding of the efforts that Savarkar and his dedicated group of people were making to unmask the insidious designs of the British. What Savarkar had started in India and carried vigorously in London was the struggle for independence of his motherland for which he had taken an oath before his family deity. The path for this was beset with dangers, in which people had to suffer at the hands of the British: flogging, rigorous imprisonment, and physical torture in jail. What Gandhi and Nehru led later was a movement, in which even imprisonment was mild, for the prisoners were provided facilities that the prisoners in the Cellular Jail could not even dream of. In a way, this easier version of the movement was facilitated by the struggle and sufferings of Savarkar and his associates. And yet many amongst us tend to forget this, just because after his release from the jail he did not join the Congress Party.

The sad aspect of the narrative of Savarkar's life is that because of his ideological differences with the Congress Party, which dominated the pre- and post-independence politics of the country, he has not only been marginalized in the accounts of Indian history produced by historians who wrote from a standpoint that gave prominence to Gandhi and Nehru but has also been maligned and demonized consistently by the successive Congress governments of the country.

Nehru, in particular, always looked for opportunities to denounce Savarkar, which pained him considerably, as is clear from one of his statements: "I have no grudge against the British atrocities inflicted upon me in London, Marseilles, and Andamans [which he humorously called 'End-a-man'] for I had vividly foreseen them as early as a boy of 14 when I took an oath at the feet of our family deity *Ashtbhuja Devi* in Bhagur. My anguish deepens as I recall the sufferings and humiliation I received in Free India at the behest of the then Supremo."

"Implicate Savarkar in Gandhi's assassination,"

thundered Nehru as soon as he got the news. A little later, he said the same to Ambedkar, who coolly but confidently replied, "Jawahar, I am sorry to hear this, but let me warn you that you cannot even touch him. He has learnt to play this game of legal hide and seek with the British Scotland Yard for many years in London, and you know they dared not do anything. Desperate and frustrated, even Winston Churchill had to deport him to India. Some day here also he will go scot-free." Soon after, Ambedkar contacted L B Bhopatkar, an eminent advocate of Pune and also President, All India Hindu Mahasabha, called him to Delhi and asked him to meet him at a secluded place in South Delhi, where he apprised him of Nehru's vindictive intentions.

Bhopatkar and several other leading advocates from Madras, Calcutta, and Delhi joined to defend Savarkar, when he was tried for his complicity in Gandhi's murder. Ambedkar's words came true on February 10, 1950, when Savarkar was exonerated honourably and Justice Atmacharan regretfully called the whole affair "sad and unfortunate."

Unlike his own country, which he struggled to liberate, the country that used all the possible fair and foul means to punish him for his actions, gave him his due when the Greater London Council took part in the worldwide celebrations of his birth centenary in 1983 and recognized his genius and ardent patriotism. In another event, on June 8, 1986, after a brief meeting in the Conference Hall of the British Parliament, several parliamentarians paid touching tributes to Savarkar.

This event was followed by another ceremony in which the Greater London Council decorated India House with a Blue Plaque—the highest social honour—and hailed Savarkar as a "Patriot and Philosopher." It was attended by several statesmen, ambassadors, and social celebrities. The ceremony was presided over by the veteran politician and statesman, Lord Fenner Brockway. Though 97, he climbed several steps to reach the rostrum and standing up spoke for about fifteen minutes about the greatness and contribution of Savarkar.

In the concluding part of his emotional homage to Savarkar, he said: "Tilak I met in 1920 as I was a Member of his Reception Committee. Savarkar, of course, I never met, but whatever I have read and heard about him, I have no hitch in saying that when Savarkar was fighting here for the freedom of his motherland, the Indian National Congress had not even thought of it." [The video recording of the speech is available with the author].

It is ironical that the country he fought against has accepted that Savarkar was 'a philosopher and patriot,' but in his own motherland, some people have vilified him as a traitor, overlooking a truth that is too patent to stare us in the face all the time: that he and his family dedicated their lives to the cause of India's freedom with single-minded devotion, for which there is no parallel in the history of India. Because of this, in his book on Savarkar, Vidya Sagar Anand observes that to forget the likes of Savarkar, who consecrated their lives to the cause of Indian nationhood, "is to throw away a vital part of our Indian national heritage." Unfortunately, that is what has happened; this vital part has suffered neglect for too long.

Tailpiece

It was on July 3, 1911 when Savarkar was brought to the Andamans to complete his two life imprisonments of twenty-five years each. He was heavily guarded and chained, handcuffed, cross-fettered and dumped into a dark and damp hellhole of 7×7 with a double enclosure.

He was given a seer of water (for all his needs, including toilet and bath) and one meal a day, and a coarse blanket to sleep on. Yoked to an oil-squeezing machine, he had to produce thirty pounds of oil every day. For shortfall of every kilo, he had to get a lash on his bare back. He could write only one letter during one year and he had to finish writing it in one hour and it was subjected to censorship. Between 1911 and 1921, he could write only eleven letters. During the same period, he scribbled 12000 lines of prose and poetry on the walls of his cell by using his nails and pebbles and memorized them. All of them were dedicated by him to his Motherland, something that has not been done by anyone in this world.

***Savarkar in Cellular Jail :** Savarkar was sentenced to fifty years rigorous imprisonment and confined in the Devil's Island of Port Blair (something unprecedented in the political history of the world). What is truly amazing is the condition—the mental anguish and the physical tortures—in which he wrote a sizeable chunk of his poetry, Yes! It is not easy to believe that some 6,000 lines of his finest poetry were composed during his two-life imprisonments in the infernal Bastille of Port Blair. Confined to his solitary cell, he would stealthily scribble his writings on the walls with nails or thorns or pins or pebbles and the like, learn them by heart and then erase them. The process went on for ten long years (1911-21), till he was repatriated to Ratnagiri, where he wrote all that he had committed to memory. Has anything in the world of letters been produced in more terrible circumstances? Perhaps not.*

Challenge

"I am not at all ambitious to become the President of India, but if I am entrusted Power, within a couple of years, I will equip India with up-to-date military might and make her stronger than even the strongest U.S.S.R. and if time demands it, I will make myself bold like Khrushchev to wave my shoe in the U.N. Assembly. No Power on the earth will then dream of offending India."

from Veer Savarkar's Speech
Poona, 16-1-61

Situated at 65, Cromwell Avenue, Highgate, North London, Savarkar's India House 'The House of Terror', 'The House of Mystery', 'The Beehive' or 'The Volcano' as the Scotland yard and the British Press branded it (Author standing outside it)

India House after the blue plaque ceremony

Senior Parliamentarian Lord Fenner Brockway unveiling a Memorabilia of Veer Savarkar at India House at 65, Cromwell Avenue, London (where Savarkar lived) on 8 June, 1985.

(Report p. 19)

Contents

Chapter 1

A Short Biographical Sketch

Savarkar was born in village Bhagur, near Nasik, on May 28, 1883. As a growing child, he was introduced by his father to the great epics of the country, *Ramayana* and *Mahabharata*, the Greek epics and plays, and some great Marathi poets. This shaped his sensibility and inspired him to write both prose and poetry in Marathi, which appeared in the newspapers of the day, when he was barely twelve.

Savarkar also displayed acute sensitivity to the happenings in the Poona of his day, especially the series of events during the momentous year of 1897, in which the city witnessed the sessions of the Indian National Congress, reverberated with the controversies generated by the Social Conference, and partook of the celebrations of Shivaji. This was followed by the sensational execution of the three Chapekar brothers—Damodar (26), Vasudev (23), and Balkrishna (19)—who were involved in the assassination of the two British plague commissioners Ryand and Ayerest, in Pune, on June 22, 1897.

The death of the brothers in the prime of their youth had a profound effect on Savarkar. In the presence of his family deity, *Ashtubuja Devi*, he sought the help of the Goddess in his efforts to follow the path of the three brothers to fight the British. He took a vow to dedicate his life to the cause of the emancipation of his motherland—the earliest vow taken by an Indian to liberate his motherland and the first of its kind taken at the tender age of fourteen—and stood by it to the best of his ability.

As the first expression of this awakened self, he wrote a spirited ballad, called *pohwara* in Marathi, in honour of the martyred brothers. When his father read it, he was shaken and also disturbed, because his response was too mature for his age and could get him into trouble, but Savarkar was not afraid of the consequences of his thoughts and actions.

When Savarkar recited the poem to his friends, they were suffused by its pathos but also felt invigorated to follow in the footsteps of the martyred brothers.

Though beset with family tragedy, because he lost his father in the plague that had spread in his village, Savarkar stood by his resolve to carry forward the work that he had promised to his family deity.

In 1899, Savarkar took the first major step in this direction by forming a group called *Mitra Mela*, which eventually became a body of the first revolutionaries from the western part of the country. The group became actively engaged in arranging lectures and meetings in which revolutionary doctrines were disseminated to young children, especially from schools. The entire city felt and responded to the activities of the group with fervour, and its growing influence was read by the British government as a threat to their presence. So the group was put under watch.

From Nasik, Savarkar moved to Poona to join Fergusson College, from where he carried forward his work with great zeal and vigour. He became a voracious reader, turned into a powerful orator and attracted people towards him. All the societies and associations of the College felt the impact of his oratorical skills. He was also able to organize a group whose members met in a secluded place, where he infused the new spirit of rebellion against the British in their young minds. The rise in its members and the buzz that it created in the corridors of the College sounded alarm bells to its authorities. His teachers gave him warning signals of the dangers he was courting, but these had no effect on him.

Under the strong influence of the proven patriotism of leaders like Shivaji, Mazzini and Garibaldi, he had set himself on a course that could not be stopped by anybody. He became known by his striking personality, his vigorous writings, and his leadership of the revolutionary movement.

A host of events inside and outside the country—the rise of Balgangadhar Tilak and Lala Lajpat Rai, the partition of Bengal, and the victories of Japan on land and sea—not only bred resentment against the British but also stirred hope that they could be fought successfully. Savarkar held on strongly to this hope, and worked hard to sharpen his skills and actions to show signs of fighting the British.

The first major show of defiance organized by him was to instil in people a strong dislike for foreign goods and love for what was produced in the country. For this he organized the striking event of burning English clothing in public. The idea was so novel and daring that even a seasoned politician like Tilak was not sure that it would work. But Savarkar made it work. He addressed several meetings to arouse people to make a bonfire of such clothing, and they did that successfully.

This bonfire on October 7, 1905 was the first of its kind in the country, and happened sixteen years before Gandhi used it as a strategy against the British on July 11, 1921 in Bombay, though many historians still give credit to him for doing this for the first time. The rousing speeches of Tilak and Paranjape on the occasion added fuel to this fire, which reverberated for many days.

The College authorities were unnerved by the response of the public and the press to the incident, which was truly novel for the times. They wanted to make sure that such incidents were not repeated and resorted to punitive action. They fined Savarkar rupees ten for his involvement in the incident and rusticated him from the college residencies within twenty-four hours.

The action taken by the College was resented by the public, and the press too condemned it. Tilak's *Kesari* opposed it vehemently in the three editorials that he wrote on October 17 and 24 and on November 17. He lashed at the academic community of the college and called it unworthy of being called *gurus*, for they could teach Shakespeare and Bacon all right but could never applaud the spirit of patriotism. As a result of this, public resentment spread to many other places as well. Savarkar's action was lauded by the public at large and a special fund was created to enable him to pay the fine imposed on him. Since the amount collected far exceeded the amount needed, Savarkar donated the excess amount to an industrial fund.

Since the expulsion of Savarkar had taken place at the very end of the session, Bombay University allowed him to take the examination, which he passed successfully, and for which he was congratulated widely by people.

Freed from the burdens of classes and schedules, Savarkar devoted all his time and energy to organizational work. He called a meeting of the societies that he had started at different places. Their members were also joined by the members of similar societies that had come up in other places as well. Savarkar addressed them with an electrifying speech and made them take a vow that the activities would not be confined to Maharashtra but extended to other states too.

All these societies merged to form one big society—*Abhinava Bharat*. Much later, its branches were established in many other parts of the world—England, France, America, Germany, Japan, and Singapore. Its goal was to make India independent, by spreading awareness among the masses and inspiring them to fight for it.

Although he kept himself busy with his activities that he thought he owed to his country, through his writings and organizing functions against the British, Savarkar did not neglect his studies. When he learnt about the scholarships that were instituted by Shyamji Krishnavarma in England for Indian students for pursuing higher studies there, he saw in this an opportunity to see and know the land of the oppressors, which could help in sharpening his fight against them.

The scholarships had two conditions attached to them that suited Savarkar's spirit: the recipients were not to take a government job on their return and they were to devote their energies to work for the liberation of their country. He wrote to Shyamji Krishnavarma that the sole motive of his life right from his schooldays was to work for his country and he would continue to do that after completing his education. Tilak recommended his application and so did B. Paranjape. By then, Savarkar was married to the daughter of Chiplunkar, who assured him of financial support to pursue his studies in London.

It is significant that by now, because of his activities and growing influence, the government had already recognized Savarkar as a threat to its power and authority, and seriously considered arresting him. But when it became known that he had won a scholarship to study in London, which would see him out of the country, and hopefully deflect his attention from his activities, it stopped. But people in the government did not know about the vow that had determined the course of his life. The administrators also underestimated the strength of his character.

Savarkar's stay in London at India House changed its very character: from a place to stay for its inmates it changed into a home that stimulated thoughts for freeing their home in India from the British yoke. Savarkar initiated a host of activities and turned the inmates into a strong well-motivated powerhouse of action. Within a few months, the impact of his programmes and his leadership became widely known and felt, which attracted the notice of the government there and became the cause of his numerous trials.

We have already stated how Gandhi and Nehru adopted British ways in London and kept themselves away from the groups of young Indians who were busy working for the freedom of their country, but Savarkar undertook his task with a commitment and vigour for which there are very few parallels. We get an early glimpse of this in his conversation with a fellow passenger Harnam Singh, during his journey to London by S S Morea, on June 9, 1906.

Savarkar's fellow traveller was a young man from a rich Punjabi family, with whom he became friendly during their stay on the ship. One day Harnam surprised him by telling him that he planned to get off at Aden to return to his mother, because being away from her made him lonely. Savarkar dissuaded him from doing that by telling him that "Our mother is dear. But dearer by far is, and ought to be, our motherland, the mother of the mothers of our race." For her, he needed to go to London, to know what the world is like, to understand the weaknesses of their masters, and to learn how to organize a Revolution and win back their lost freedom. Hearing him speak like a true patriot, the young man changed his mind and decided to continue with his journey to London.

Most of the activities that Savarkar undertook in London and the dangers he courted because of this have been stated in a shortened form in his first trial that forms Chapter 2 of this book.

The fact, though not always understood in its true spirit, is that the activities of the revolutionaries put a sustained pressure on the government both in England and India in granting concessions to the Indians, in the form of reforms. Writing to the *London Times* from Bombay in January 1909, Sir Valentine Chirol stated: "I detect a general tendency to ascribe these lavish gifts to the vigorous actions of the extremists. If it had not been for the bombs, we should not have had these boons, was a remark which roughly summed up the popular opinion in this aspect of the subject."

The London trial also exposed the double standards of the British judicial system. The very fact that Savarkar was tried in London under a law that was formulated in India and did not apply to him at all shows that they were not inclined to judge him fairly. Even then, as a face-saving strategy, the court decreed that he be tried once again, in India, which became the basis of the Nasik trial, which is dealt with in its fullness in Chapter 3.

When Savarkar was being transported to India, the ship carrying him stopped at the French port of Marseilles. There, too, the British violated the norms of international law by arresting him on the French soil. The verdict given by the tribunal at the Hague, that was constituted to decide on the issue of his asylum, showed the international body in a poor light. The details about that figure in Chapter 4.

Because the verdict in the Hague trial went in favour of England, the decision on Savarkar's deportation to the Andamans became effective. He accepted his double life imprisonment with calm resignation. When he was about to board the train for Madras for his departure to the Andamans, one of the British officers told him: "I will never forget this your dignified courage."

Between these three trials and the last one that he faced in the post-independence times, there is a long interval of time. Quite a sizable part of it was spent by Savarkar in the prison at the Cellular Jail. One has only to read to believe the kind of hardships that prisoners were subjected to there and the physical and mental sufferings that they had to undergo.

Dhananjay Keer, an early biographer of Savarkar, writes about the terrible conditions of the life of revolutionaries in the prison thus:

> ...[they] had to undergo unbearable physical tortures. They were yoked to the oil-mill. And the working on the oil-mill demanded such hard labour that it squeezed the life even out of the hardened and seasoned convicts, and they trembled at its sight. The oil-mill was, therefore, aptly regarded as the friend of suicide. Prisoners had to turn its handle horizontally for hours together without even a slight break. They had to take their meals and drink water, while the oil mill was in motion lest the quota of the oil should fall below the expectation. Even with such hard labour full measure of the required quota could never be fulfilled by even the strongest prisoner. Their hands bled; hearts ached; heads whirled. They fell in dead faints. When they revived, round and round they had to go again in excruciating agony.

Savarkar withstood all the hardships of the prison life with stoic forbearance. During the toughest moments of his toils, he kept his mind free from what he was doing and immersed himself in his roving imagination. In one of his annual letters written from the prison, he writes that "While my hands and feet are automatically doing the given task, my spirit avoiding all determination is out for a morning trip, and across the seas and oceans, over hills and dales, it roams sipping only pleasant things and things noble, like a bee among flowers. Then I compose some new lines."

Unlike most of the later-day political prisoners, who spent their time in the prison in India to write books, because they were supplied with writing materials, Savarkar had to spend his time doing brutal hard work during the day and spend his night in a cell with hardly any facilities. Because of this, he composed everything in his head and transferred that onto the walls of his cell by using thorns and pebbles, and then stored them in his memory. In this way, he was able to create some ten thousand lines of poetry in Marathi, which he got published later, and for which he earned lavish praise from discerning critics about their literary excellence.

Considering that Savarkar was a force to reckon with, even when he was in prison and far away from the shores of his country, the British made several attempts to grant him freedom on the condition that he would collaborate with them. Sir Reginald Craddock visited the Andamans to persuade him to earn his freedom by restraining the activities of his colleagues in India and abroad, to which he did not agree.

At the end of World War I, a vigorous campaign was launched by several influential individuals, political leaders and the press to plead with the British to release all the political prisoners held by the British in different jails. In fact, some people like Ananatarao Gadre, Senapati Bapat, and Shivrampant Paranjape collected thousands of signatures on a petition for the release of prisoners, and it met with success. The Royal Proclamation on this was issued on December 24, 1919, but it specifically mentioned that clemency has to be "compatible with public safety." Because the British feared Savarkars, for Vinayak's brother too was a prisoner there, they were excluded from the list of the released, even though many prisoners from the Cellular Jail and many who had come there after their imprisonment were included. Several other attempts to seek their release were made by leaders like Patel and Tilak, in 1920 and 1921, but with no success.

In 1921, K V Rangaswamy Ayyangar moved a resolution in the Council of State recommending to the Governor-General-in-Council to extend amnesty to Savarkar. That was accepted, but he and his brother had still to stay in the Alipore Jail in India. So more requests for his unconditional release were made by Ratnagiri political Conference and by a resolution of the Indian National Congress held in Cocanada, held in 1923.

Because of these efforts, Savarkar was released conditionally on January 6, 1924, from Yeravda Jail. The conditions were: (a) that he had to reside within the district of Ratangiri, and that he could leave the place only in severe emergency and with the permission of the Government; (b) for five years he was not to take part in any political activity, and the decision in this regard would be reconsidered after the expiry of that period.

Debarred from taking part in any political activity, Savarkar used his time and energy to concentrate on social activities related to his community and on enriching the Marathi language and its literature.

Since the Congress Party had accepted separate electorates for the Muslims, Savarkar thought it appropriate that he should work towards consolidating the Hindus and introducing reforms in the society to rid it of its ugly sores that had divided it into castes and sub-castes, creating a huge web of inequalities and strife within its fold. In doing that, he was also being realistic and responding to the need of the times. This is clarified in his meeting with Shaukat Ali. When he came to meet Savarkar in November 1924, he praised his patriotism, but expressed his disapproval of the work he did for his *sanghattan*. Savarkar told him point blank that if he would stop his involvement with the Khilafat, he too would stop doing what he was doing. He told him that there should be no separate organizations for the two communities. Since that was not to be, Savarkar started a non-political organisation, Hindu Mahasabha, with the express intention of reforming the Hindu society. In this, he was much ahead of many other leaders of his day.

Even while doing that, Savarkar worked towards promoting mutual respect within the communities. On the days of Hindu festivals, he visited the Muslim and Christian quarters, but these visits were not reciprocated.

On top of the list of his reform agenda was his fight against the sanatanists, for their opposition to mixed schools, that is, schools where students from all the castes could come to learn. Savarkar's argument was simple and yet so telling: if the upper castes were willing to treat the lower castes equals when they came before them in their converted *avatar* of Christians or Muslims, why should they not treat them as equals before they move out of their original fold to embrace these new faiths.

It was in this context that Savarkar wrote about reconversions, which many people, including the nationalist Congressmen dubbed communal and anti-national. His logic was simple: reconversions happen only because there are conversions. If conversions are stopped, reconversions will stop automatically. He was compelled to stress this because Muslim leaders, even within the fold of the Congress Party, made proclamations about conversions, and nobody criticized them or opposed them.

Two prominent examples of such proclamations can be cited from around this time. Mohamad Ali, speaking from the presidential chair of the Indian National Congress openly said that the depressed classes of the country should be divided equally between the Hindus and Muslims, and yet he was neither communal nor anti-national. Another Muslim leader Yakub Hassan went a step further. In the address he presented to Gandhi, he openly told the Muslims to convert all the untouchables in India to Islam, and yet he was a patriotic person.

Savarkar felt that changing people's thinking about the removal of caste barriers was not enough to produce any concrete gains. This had to be translated into action.

Starting mixed schools was one such action, but that did not touch the lives of many people. So he chose to target the most important activity of the Hindus, in which everybody was involved: going to the temples. Because of the caste restrictions that had been observed for centuries, people from the lower castes were not allowed to go into temples. The upper castes feared that their touch would contaminate them. Savarkar's argument against this was simple and forceful. If people did not hate to touch animals like dogs and cats, then why hate to touch beings of their own kind?

To overcome this age-old prejudice, Savarkar changed the very character of the popular Ganesh festival; he made it into a pan-Hindu festival in which people from all castes were allowed to participate. Slowly, he created room for the lower castes to enter into the temples that they had not been allowed to enter. He started by opening the Vithoba temple for them. The lower castes took to reading Vedas, and singing Vedic hymns. He presided over the *sabhas* where these were sung.

To extend it further, Savarkar inspired Bhagoji Baloji Keer to raise a new temple in Ratnagiri, which was named *Patit Pavan* temple. It was thrown open to all the Hindus on February 22, 1931, at a meeting held under the chairmanship of Shankaracharya, who was garlanded on the occasion by a *harijan*. The temple had priests from all the classes, who delivered sermons, and people from all the castes and classes met freely.

To reinforce the cementing of bonds between people from different castes, Savarkar also encouraged the practice of their eating together, *sahabhojan*. One such public *bhoj* was organized in 1930. It drew the attention of a wide spectrum of people, including the politicians. The *Times of India* of December 9, 1930, stated that this happening has "given deep offence to Nationalist Congressmen, who are believers along with Gandhi in four watertight castes by birth."

In attacking inequalities among the Hindus, Savarkar was far ahead of the people of his times, including Gandhi, and declared emphatically: "I shall eat with any Hindu irrespective of caste. I shall not believe in caste by birth or by profession and henceforth I shall call myself a Hindu only—not Brahmin, Vaishya, etc."

Well versed in the intricacies of human mind, Savarkar was equally conscious of the fact that the lower castes were not too ready to accept these radical ideas and practices. That is why he felt the need to tell them that "your weakness is worse than the wickedness of the caste Hindus.... Be men. Know that you are men.... Live a clean and temperate life.... Never disown your fathers, saints, and blood. Do not observe untouchability among yourselves.... That is also your duty. Forget it not."

Apart from social concerns, Savarkar also devoted his time to the development of Marathi language and literature. He wrote poems, plays, novels and histories in Marathi. Notable works included *Pad-Padshahi*, which dealt with the rise and fall of the Maratha Empire and a book based on his prison experiences, *My Transportation of Life*, which was proscribed by the government. He also worked to purify the Marathi language.

Though Savarkar was busy with his social work, the British kept a careful watch on him and went on extending his confinement. At times, they tried to cook up excuses to implicate him in subversive activities. On one occasion, the police came to his home to search for copies of the book that was proscribed even before it saw the light of day, *Indian War of Independence of 1857*, and found none. Another incident is quite amusing. In 1934, he was arrested because shots had been fired by somebody at a military officer in Bombay.

Attempts to get him released continued to be made by individuals and organizations. One such attempt was made in July 1935 by Dr M B Velkar who set up a Savarkar Restriction Committee under his chairmanship. To lend weight to his efforts, he approached Gandhi for help, but, to his utter surprise, he told him that he did not know who Savarkar was and that he thought it derogatory to approach the British government for his release. When he went to Nehru to seek his help, Nehru looked at the paper given to him and tore it to bits. So Savarkar's release had to wait for two more years. He was finally released on May 10, 1937 only when Jamna Das Mehta made his release a precondition for forming the provincial government.

Soon after his release, Savarkar made it known that it was quite legitimate that people should have different views on how to realize the aim of freeing India, and they should work with a spirit of accommodation and goodwill. "The object of our worship, he said, "is the Goddess of Freedom. The temple is one. Let the ways and means differ. The worshippers should not quarrel among themselves over the means. Differences always exist and the clashes make for light." To provide a ready example, he said that Tilak, Gokhale, and Surendranath Banerjee had different views on the question of fighting for the freedom of the country, but they did not consider politicians of independent thinking their enemies.

Now that Savarkar had the freedom to choose his political path, he joined Tilak's Democratic Swaraj Party, but later joined the Hindu Mahasabha. He could have joined the Indian National Congress and because of the sacrifices that he had already made for his country and also because of his intellectual acumen and oratorical skills, he could have risen high in its ranks, but he did not do that. In his view, the Congress had deviated from its patriotic and nationalistic ideals. He took a particular exception to Congress's attitude towards the Muslims, the manner in which it had started appeasing them, though they had already found leaders from within their community to plead their cause.

Savarkar felt that Gandhi had turned anti-Hindu. Because the Maharaja of Kashmir presided over a Muslim-majority state, Gandhi advised him to leave his throne in favour of the Muslims, but did not find it necessary to give such advice to the Nizam of Hyderabad and the Nawab of Bhopal who ruled Hindu majority states. This sharpened Savarkar's resolve to carve out his philosophy of *Hindutava,* which he distinguished from Hinduism. *Hindutava* is a cultural term that stands for a common culture, common history, common language, and common country.

Savarkar went on a whirlwind tour of the country and kept on clarifying his stand and his position *vis-à-vis* other parties and leaders. In May 1938, he spoke before the press in Lahore to tell its representatives that he was different from Jinnah, because "he stood for equality and no concessions [but] Jinnah did not stand for equality and always asked for more and more concessions." Savarkar told the representatives that there should be joint electorates with reservation of seats for minorities either on population basis or according to a system of weightages equally applicable to all the minorities. He further said that the Congress should assume the role of a Parliament in which all parties should participate, and not that of a party, as it was developing in those days.

The Congress was tested in 1938 and found wanting when trouble arose in Hyderabad because the Hindus rose in revolt against the tyrannical ways of the Nizam. They were barred from holding meetings, religious as well as political; they could not repair their temples; they could not give their children the education of their choice; and what was worse, they watched helplessly the Muslims control eighty per cent of jobs. The Congress did nothing to help the downtrodden Hindus. The Nizam relented only because of the perseverance of the agitators and the pressure that Arya Samaj and All India Hindu Mahasabha exerted on him.

It is ironic that Savarkar's plea to the Congress to be accommodative, to take along with them parties that differed from them in their outlook and thinking, resulted in an action that shocked such parties and compelled them to come together to express their pain and anguish by passing a resolution against the Congress. The action taken by the Congress was unprecedented, for it boycotted the Hindu Mahasabha, little realizing that by doing that it was sharpening the Hindu-Muslim divide that the British had been working for.

Soon after this, in Bombay, Sir Cowasji Jehangir, Sir Chimanlal Setalvad, and Sir V R Chandravarkar, on behalf of Indian Liberals, N C Kelkar and Jamna Das Mehta on behalf of the Democratic Swaraj Party, Dr B R Ambedkar on behalf of the Independent Labour Party, and Savarkar on behalf of the Hindu Mahasabha issued a statement, which was a significant comment on the culture of the Congress Party: "The Congress and the Congress Governments believe in annihilating all parties and making the Congress the only party on the land, as is the case in Fascist and Nazi regimes—a result which would be a death-blow to democracy."

This is reflected in their actions, too. Though the Act of 1935 was accepted, the Federal Part of the Act was not adopted at all. Jinnah had all the reasons for making statements against it and condemning it, because he knew that it would provide for a strong and unified India, but the Congress had no reason for this, unless they wanted to save themselves from his anger. Jinnah went to the extent of saying that the Western form of democracy did not suit the Muslim interests, for this would turn them into a minority. They did not want to be a minority, but a separate nation.

Because of these conditions, in which Muslims were all the time dictating terms both to the Congress and the British, Savarkar was compelled to find ways to strengthen the Hindus. In meeting after meeting, in different parts of the country, he urged them to join the military and use the training for safeguarding the freedom of their country. It was also necessary to do that because the Muslims had monopolised the army and constituted nearly three-fourths of the Indian army.

Apart from initiating radical changes in the Hindu social structure and advocating the militarization of the community, Savarkar also formulated his idea of *Hindutva*, which has generated a lot of debate and discussion in our times. He made a careful distinction between nation and state. First, he said that "every person is a Hindu who regards his *Bharat Bhumi*—this land from India to the seas, as his Fatherland and Holyland—the land of origin of his religion and the cradle of his faith." Thus it is clear that it is not a religious dogma or creed. Since Muslims did not consider the country as their Holyland, they miss out on being part of the nation. Because of this, they and people from other communities are minorities.

To make sure that these people are rightfully accommodated within the country, Savarkar conceived the idea of the Indian state, in which all citizens, irrespective of caste, creed, race or religion are treated alike on the principle of "one man one vote."

Savarkar also denounced the idea of absolute non-violence, for he considered it unrealistic. For it does not work in a world in which evil exists along with good, and where people are both fair and unfair. In fact, the possibility of violence helps in creating hope for destroying evil and letting justice prevail. "Because every evil-doer has his avenger, there is still some hope in the heart of the world that injustice cannot last." It is because of this that he regretted the change of the firebrand Sarojini Naidu into a parrot of Gandhi, of her going back on what she herself had said in the Lucknow session of the Indian National Congress: "...the refusal of the privilege, that gifted privilege and inalienable right to carry arms, is to insult the very core of their valiant manhood."

Savarkar clinches his argument by stating that even the saints had recommended that violence became necessary in specific situations. Saint Tukaram, for example, said: "Kill the scorpion, the despiser of the worship of God, if it enters the shrine; give tit for tat. No mercy to the wicked."

Savarkar had to bear with another shocking revelation. On April 12, 1943, Rajgopalachari, speaking on the birthday of the Prophet, spoke about the granting of Pakistan to the Muslims, though Jinnah said soon after that the proposal of Gandhi was not fair to them. When Rajgopalachari admitted that he had been working on the proposal for two years and "I had secured Gandhi's unqualified support to the scheme and it conceded all that the Muslim League had ever demanded in its resolution of 1940," it became sufficiently clear that the partition had been agreed to years before it actually happened, and that Gandhi was privy to it.

All that Savarkar could do at this time was to ask Hindus to observe the first week of August 1944 as the United India and anti-Pakistan week. He also organized demonstrations against it, but soon after, ill health and the death of his brother Babu Rao virtually put an end to his active involvement in the affairs of the country.

The hostility of the Congress towards the Hindu Mahasabha continued, and largely because of this, it was dropped from the Shimla Conference that was held in June 1945. The Wavell Plan that put the caste Hindus and Muslims on parity was so unjust that the Hindu Mahasabha, once again, observed a protest week, but it did not resort to direct action, which could have made a difference.

Because of his ill health, Savarkar distanced himself from political activities. But on the day of the country's independence, though saddened by its division, he unfurled the new flag of the country along with the flag of the united India. He also consented to Dr Mookerjee's joining the national cabinet.

Savarkar was also witness to needless controversies created by Gandhi and Nehru whether or not the country should be called Hindustan. Nehru had to concede in October 1947 that the "Congress wanted to establish a secular democratic state in the country. Naturally in such a state the predominant culture and outlook would be governed by the great majority of the Hindus in the population."

The violence that followed the partition of the country exposed Gandhi's unrealistic concept of non-violence. He came under fire from all quarters, including some of his trusted friends. Frustrated by Gandhi's thinking and actions, Nathuram Godse assassinated him on January 30, 1948. This led to massive violence in Bombay against the Hindu Mahasabha leaders and Savarkar's arrest from his house. The details of his arrest and the trial that followed are given in Chapter 5 of this book.

We only want to add here that even after he was freed honourably by the court, he was not allowed to leave the Red Fort. By another order he was prohibited from entering Delhi for three months and escorted to Bombay under police protection. To avoid his contact with the public, his movements were kept secret.

As if this was not enough, he was, once again, arrested in Bombay on April 4, 1950 under Preventive Detention Act, because Liaqat Ali Khan was to visit Delhi to meet Nehru on his invitation. The reason given was that he was inciting the Hindus against the Muslims. He was released on July

13, only after giving an undertaking that he would not participate in political activities and remain confined to his own house in Bombay.

Another fact that needs to be mentioned here is that the ban imposed on his books by the British continued up to 1953, although the country became free in 1947. Some of his books were translated into Hindi after that only because of the efforts of Dr Rajendra Prasad and Lal Bahadur Shastri.

Savarkar passed away on February 26, 1966, by *Atma-arpana*—an ancient practice followed by our *rishis*—of offering one's soul (*atma*) to the super-soul (*paramatma*) The Golden Jubilee of this event was celebrated with great zeal and fervour at hundreds of places in India and many other parts of the world on February 26, 2016.

❑

Chapter 2
Savarkar's Trial in England

Savarkar was brought to trial in London in 1910, in Bowstreet Court, during the last year of his eventful stay of five years in the city. The trial is a tangled web of colonial machinations and a sordid mixture of deceit, treachery, and betrayal. It was manipulated by the British to create the basis for another trial of Savarkar in India, known as the Nasik conspiracy case.

Before he came to London, Savarkar was a bright student, full of verve and enthusiasm, and totally committed to working for the liberation of his motherland. Fortunately for him, he was able to compete successfully for a scholarship to study in England, instituted by another lover of freedom, Shyamji Krishnavarma, who, after getting educated at Cambridge and Oxford, returned to India for a brief while, but went back to settle in England.

To help Indian students who were desirous of studying in England, Krishnavarma set up scholarships in the name of great Indians: Swami Dayanand, Rana Partap, Shivaji, and many more. Since Savarkar hailed from Maharashtra, he applied for the Shivaji scholarship, for which he was strongly recommended by Bal Gangadhar Tilak and B Paranjape, the editor of *Kal*.

The manner in which Savarkar put forth his claim as a worthy candidate for this scholarship provides an insight into the working of his mind and also explains the activities that he started in England, which led to the trials that he had to face in his life:

> Independence and liberty I look upon as the very pulse and breath of the nation. From my boyhood, dear sir, up to the moment of my youth, the loss of Independence of my country and the possibility of regaining it form the only theme of which I dreamt by night and on which I mused by day.

Savarkar also satisfied Krishnavarma about the condition attached to the scholarship: that he would not accept any government job after completing his education.

In this way, Savarkar won the scholarship to study Law in London. He stayed in India House, a place that had been set up by Krishnavarma for students who came from India for higher studies. What happened there affected the turn of events in India, and what happened in India, affected the turn of events in England. This criss-crossing of events reached a point where, out of sheer desperation, the British found that they had no alternative but to arrest and try Savarkar in England, so that he could eventually be tried, sentenced, and silenced for ever in India. What follows is a short sequential account of how it came about.

Within months of his stay in London, Savarkar emerged as a natural leader of the group that lived in India House, for he used his ability and his organizational acumen to radicalize the Home Rule propaganda of peaceful revolution that had been advocated by Krishnavarma. He started "Free India Society," modelled on Mazzini's "Young Italy," but also as the English *avatar* of the society that he had already established in India, *Abhinava Bharat,* which, in his absence was being looked after by his elder brother Baba Rao Savarkar. Baba Rao was charged later for publishing a poem which started with the line of a Marathi poet Govind that "No country has won freedom without a war" and deported to the Andamans. In his speeches, Savarkar too would frequently remind people: "Remember! Freedom is neither begged nor borrowed. It is always snatched with force and fight."

The primary objective of the Society was to spread awareness among its members and the public at large that there was need for a revolutionary struggle against the British. For this purpose, he lectured to its members on the struggles that had succeeded in other parts of the world: Italy, France, and America. From among the Indian students who came from different parts of England to attend the meetings organized by the Society, he carved a special core group, *Abhinava Bharat Society,* which advocated ceaseless armed struggle against the British occupation of India.

Since the Special Department in India was fully aware of his political involvement during his student days in India, it sent a confidential letter to the British authorities at India Office in London to give them their assessment of Savarkar. In his thinking and opinions, the letter stated, he is like Damodar Chapekar, who had murdered Rand in 1897, "a firebrand to be watched." This clearly shows that the British had focussed their attention on him right from the time he had landed in England.

Impressed by Savarkar's devotion to the cause of India's freedom and his ability to arrange activities for realizing it, Krishnavarma handed over the care of India House to him and left for Paris. Prominent firebrands like Harindranath Chattopadhyaya and VVS Aiyar and several other leaders joined Savarkar in his efforts to propagate the need for working towards a revolution for liberating the country, which received impetus by the deportation from India of leaders like Lala Lajpat Rai and Bhagat Singh's uncle, Sardar Ajit Singh, who had been involved in the armed struggle for over four decades.

The group initiated measures for widening the scope of the activities of the Society. With the help of a Russian exile, its members put together a manual for making bombs, which was sent to important locations in India where, with the help of volunteers sent from England, these were tried out for use.

To add fuel to this new awakening, Savarkar translated Mazzini's writings into Marathi and got them published in Nasik. As anticipated by him, it produced the desired result of drawing the attention of his countrymen and women to fight the British. The book had a record sale, was widely reviewed, and promptly proscribed.

Savarkar followed it up with another book, *Indian War of Independence: 1857*, which was about the events that took place in that year in India, and were labelled by the British as the mutiny of 1857. Savarkar's book was meant to promote a new understanding of the efforts of the people who had been branded unprincipled rogues and fanatics by the British. Anticipating its threatening impact on the people of India, the British proscribed it even before it was fully written. When the book was completed, Savarkar's revolutionary friends, who were active in Europe and England, smuggled it into India by using ingenious methods of hiding it behind fictional titles like *Pickwick Papers* and the novels of Walter Scott. Madam Cama smuggled a copy from Holland to London in her sari in 1908.

Savarkar wanted to draw the attention of the public to the efforts of their predecessors to fight the British and to charge their imagination to continue that fight by using violent means.

When the British organized functions in London in 1907 to celebrate the fiftieth anniversary of their victory in 1857, by ridiculing the people who had fought them as mutineers, Krishnavarma did something spectacular. He drew attention to what had happened in that year by publishing a strongly worded letter of his Irish friend, Hugh O'Donnell, entitled "A Triple Reparation."

Describing the happenings of those days as "tragic events," O'Donnell wanted the government headed by Lord Minto to associate itself with the grief and indignation of the millions of Indians, but he hardly knew that the British did not look at the events of those tragic times from his lens. Given the nature of the political governance in India, the British were least inclined to do such a thing and would not permit any Indian organization to do anything of the kind.

Since the repressive regime of the British India had no jurisdiction over London, Savarkar organized a campaign of counter-commemoration to honour the people who had taken part in it: Nana Sahib, Tatya Tope, Jhansi Rani, Maulavi Ahmed Saheb and many others. Pamphlets were printed and distributed to educate the general public about what had actually happened in that year and how the British were looking at the events and people involved in them from an anti-people perspective.

Because of this and also because of the relentless campaign of Savarkar to intensify efforts at arousing the consciousness of different sections of the Indian society, through his writings, the activities of India House came under the direct scrutiny of the Scotland Yard.

Whatever happened in London could not but impact the political climate in India. The *Abhinava Bharat* of Maharashtra too came under the direct gaze of the British, who believed that its members received arms, explosives and inflammatory literature from Savarkar. Savarkar's eldest brother was arrested in connection with riots in Nasik and Bombay. For leading a mob in Bombay, he was sentenced to rigorous imprisonment for six months.

Later, Savarkar's brother was also arrested for waging war against the British King, because he had helped in publishing a poem that had cited examples to show that no country can attain independence without waging war against its aggressor. His house was also searched, in which the police found documents advocating war and manuals for making explosives. Because of this, he was sentenced to transportation for life. His appeal against the verdict was dismissed and the sentence confirmed.

The British administration in India had hoped that its action against Savarkar's brothers and relatives would dampen his spirit and he would desist from actions that he had been indulging in relentlessly to strengthen his campaign to free his country by using force, and motivating young people to join the ranks of such people. But Savarkar was made of a different mettle; he could not be cowed down by what the British did to his family members. He wrote a touching consolatory letter in the form of a poem to his sister-in-law, in which he expressed tender sentiments, but also pleaded with the Almighty to grant him strength to shoulder the "momentous responsibility" of continuing with his efforts to work for the freedom of his country.

The happenings in India and England were getting tangled up. What happened in one location affected happenings in another location. What happened in India was the direct result of colonial oppression, which became severe because of the resistance shown by the Indian people. These produced a violent reaction in Britain. And that is how this process continued.

The worst part of these complex interactions was that the streak of oppression in London became visible even in places that were normally outside the fold of political influence and hence least expected. In spite of spending his time and energy in organizing anti-British activities, Savarkar did not neglect his studies, and cleared all the examinations that qualified him to be called to the Bar, but the Benchers of the Grays's Inn framed a case against him and put him on trial. Coming under fire from the local press for arrogating to themselves the powers that vested in the courts, the members relented, but put a condition on him for getting permission to practice law: to give an undertaking that he would desist from taking part in revolutionary activities. But because he did not do that, he was not admitted to the Bar and thus not allowed to practice law.

In *The Times of India* of July 21, 1994, Bhaskar Ghorpade reported from London that he had succeeded in finding details about the work of the committee that was appointed for the purpose of looking into the charges brought against Savarkar. The inquiry of the committee lasted for fifteen days and he was personally present during those days. The charges against him were discussed but "nothing could be proved" against him, and yet he was not given the license to practice for the reason stated in the previous paragraph. Because of this, Ghorpade pleaded with the Inn that "barristership" be conferred on him posthumously. That has not happened till now.

The persecution of the Indians in India fuelled the anger of young revolutionaries in England and charged them with the spirit of hitting at the ruling class. This culminated in the assassination of Curzon Wylie by Madan Lal Dhingra. Though it shone brightly as a patriotic act, some Indians, including Dhingra's father and brothers, acted treacherously like toadies, and condemned it in very strong terms.

Gandhi too was in London around this time, as the member of a delegation from South Africa. Like Dhingra's brothers, he too mourned the loss of Wylie, and called Dhingra's act "cowardly" and "childish," and a polluted act, the result of "ill-digested reading of worthless writings." The most ironic part of this is that even though leaders like Winston Churchill considered this an act of heroism, like that of "Plutarch's immortal heroes," Gandhi spoke about it disparagingly as one of "childishness." He went to the extent of stating that Dhingra's defence reflected only his "mental derangement," and the people who had incited him, which was a clear reference to Savarkar, "will be called to account in God's court and are also guilty in the eyes of the world and deserve to be punished."

Many such people living in London thought that Dhingra's action should be condemned publicly. On July 5, they hastily called a meeting for the purpose at Caxton Hall. Betraying the cause of freedom of their country, speaker after speaker rose to condemn the act and then one of them moved a resolution to that effect and declared it passed unanimously. Just then, Savarkar broke the silence and said that since he was against the resolution, it could not be deemed to have been passed unanimously. When the people present there found who he was, they got furious. One of them gave him a hard blow, which broke his glasses and injured his eye. With blood flowing from his wound, he repeated in his calm voice: "In spite of this all I still vote against this resolution."

This led to a scuffle between the pro- and anti-British people. Savarkar reined in his supporters, and let the police do its job. He was taken to the police station, but freed after about an hour. The police expressed regret over the happening and offered to take into custody the person who had attacked him, if he so wished. But Savarkar told them that he did not want that, because he had already got his reward. But to prove that he was right and the people who had gathered to condemn the event and indulged in violence against him were wrong, he wrote a letter to the *Times* about the incident, which they duly published.

The attitude of the police regarding the incident and the readiness of the *Times* to publish his letter was a clear recognition of his right to dissent, an important aspect of the liberal British society. This encouraged Savarkar to continue with his efforts to work for the liberation of his motherland. But this was only one side of the picture.

Though it was true that he was in England, it was equally true that he was not a British citizen; he was an Indian subject who had constantly been challenging the British authority in India. So in the eyes of the British government, he was a dangerous person and a marked man.

Meanwhile, Dhingra's trial grabbed the headlines. Refusing to offer any defence, he delivered a powerful speech in which he stated that he had carried out the assassination to "avenge the inhuman sentences passed on Indian youths, of death and transportation for life, whose only crime was that they took up arms to free their motherland."

Savarkar wanted that a longer document that Dhingra carried on his person should also get known to the general public. Although the police tried their best to ensure that that did not happen, Savarkar managed to find a copy and got it published under the title "Challenge" and had it distributed in India, America, and England.

With the help of an Irish friend, and unknown to the editor of the paper, "Challenge" was published also in *Daily News*, and was read and admired not only by the public but also by the leading politicians of the day, as a vigorous example of patriotic sentiment. For its patriotic fervour, the very last lines of the "Challenge," which many believed were written by Savarkar himself, are worth quoting:

> The only lesson required in India at present is to learn how to die and the only way to teach it is by dying ourselves. Therefore I die and glory in my martyrdom. My only prayer to God is: may I be reborn of the same Mother and may I re-die in the same sacred cause till

the cause is successful and she stands free for the good of humanity and the glory of God.

This event sent shock waves to the government and its detective agencies. Many people, including those in the media, believed that Savarkar was the man behind all these disruptive activities. Because of this, spies started chasing Indians and India House came under their scrutiny. Life became so unbearable for the Indians living there that the place had to be closed. Left on their own, many of them found it difficult to get living accommodation, for wherever they went, the police went after them, causing harassment to the house owners.

Because the British lost their grip over conditions created by the Indians in London, their cruel ways touched abominable proportions in India. Savarkar's friends and relatives were selectively targeted. They lost their jobs and suffered persecution. When a bomb was thrown at Lord Minto in Ahmedabad, Savarkar's younger brother Narayan Rao was taken into custody as a suspect.

In London, Savarkar's life was made difficult by the spies because they shadowed him relentlessly. This proved a source of annoyance to the people who provided him lodgings. When he was forced to change three lodgings within a single day, he could not take it any more, and decided to shift to Brighton. There he regained his health and wrote a memorable sea-ode expressing longing for his home in India.

With improved health, Savarkar devoted himself to writing short pieces in which he stressed the importance of revolutionary activities for removing the fetters of his mother.

While Savarkar was there, he read about the shooting of Jackson, the Collector of Nasik, by Ananata Kanhere, who declared that he had done the deed "to avenge the sentence of transportation passed on Savarkar's brother

Baba Rao Savarkar." Because of this, several of Savarkar's friends and his brother Narayan Rao, who had been released only a few days before, were arrested again on charges of murder and waging war against the king.

The assassination created a storm in England. Many dailies wrote that all the disruptive activities in India had their origin in London and urged the authorities that all the people involved in them be brought to book. Some openly mentioned Savarkar as the man behind the violent acts and wondered why he was not being arrested.

In the wake of this surcharged atmosphere, Savarkar's friends and well-wishers were almost certain that he could be arrested any time. The leaders who were in Paris told him to leave England at once, but he refused. But when the executive members of the *Abhinava Bharat* moved a formal resolution that he should go to Paris and told Gyan Chand Varma to ensure that he did, Savarkar had to leave London. Varma saw him off at Victoria Station on January 5, 1910. In his diary, he wrote almost prophetically that that was the last he saw Savarkar as a free man.

In Paris, Savarkar stayed near the leaders who, like him, worked for India's freedom, including Madam Cama, who had unfurled the flag of independent India in Germany, in Sttutgart, on August 22, 1907, during a meeting of the International Socialist Congress. He used his stay in Paris to organize meetings to galvanize Indians to work for the independence of the country.

Very soon, Savarkar felt that he had not much to do in France. Reports from India about the hardships and torture suffered by his countrymen distressed him no end. He started reproaching himself for playing it safe in Paris and felt that he should be in India with the suffering Indians, but Krishnavarma tried to convince him that because he was a general, he was not supposed to be in the company of soldiers.

Savarkar did not accept the sound argument of Krishnavarma. He did not even accept the logic behind it, and answered him thus: "But it is only by fighting first by their side in the firing line that I can prove my worth of being exalted to the position of a general: otherwise everyone would think himself, by a deceptive notion of one's self-importance to be as indispensable as a general and thus claim to remain at the Headquarters.... Will not, moreover, this kind of argument serve the cowards as a handy shield to hide their fear?"

Savarkar knew that though he had a strong desire to be with his suffering brethren in India, he could not go there, for there he would be arrested for sure. Going back to England was a better option because the country had an established tradition of giving refuge to revolutionaries from different countries of the world, and this had been demonstrated several times in the past. He also thought that even if he was arrested, though the chances of that seemed slim at that time, because he had no connection whatsoever with the young man who had killed the Collector of Nasik, he would be tried in England. He would get a fair trial, and also an opportunity to tell the world about the sufferings of his people in India. Even though he reasoned on these lines, he still was not sure that he should return to England. He knew that he was no ordinary revolutionary; he was an Indian, who was also the foremost enemy of the British Empire, because he posed a direct challenge to its might.

Soon after he read that people involved in the Nasik trial had been sentenced, and though his brother's name did not figure in them, his conscience still pricked him. It constantly awakened him to his responsibilities, releasing the whole gamut of emotions. In fact, he envisaged his present situation as one that was meant to test him: whether or not he would be able to stand up to the pressure of the moment, which could lead to imprisonment, exile, even death. He also realized that he could ask people to join the freedom struggle against the British only if he gave evidence of his willingness and ability to suffer its consequences: "I will risk, will suffer, will myself pay the highest price—then alone I shall have the right to exhort others to risk and suffer and pay."

Having made up his mind to go back to London, he talked about this to his friends, but they were not convinced that he was right in his thinking. A letter from Aiyar from London, in which he had written that he expected him to be back soon, helped him to overcome the disapproval of his French friends. So he bade goodbye to them and left the shores of France.

After touching the British territory, Savarkar took the train to London. Inside the train, he could sense that he was being watched. This was confirmed when he found a group of detectives waiting for him at the Victoria station. This was March 13, 1910, "The ides of March, " as they know it. When they swooped on him, he demanded that they show him the warrant to arrest him. They told him that they would, and took him to a room where Inspector Parker of Scotland Yard showed him the warrant issued from India, with charges of "sedition and abetment of murder."

There are several interesting aspects to Savarkar's arrest, which clarify how carefully and meticulously the authorities had planned to ensure that he was sent to India.

The government in Britain knew that although he was vigorously involved in political propaganda, he had not overtly committed any offence against the British law and could not therefore be arrested. But because the government wanted to nail him and silence his troublesome voice, it chose a strategy that shows the evil side of colonial machinery. He was arrested by the British Police in London under a warrant issued by the Bombay High Court. Though it might sound strange, and even unreasonable and unfair, that is what the British did.

Although Savarkar had come to England as a student on a regular passport issued by the government and observed all the legal formalities for staying as a resident in London, the British government in India declared him a fugitive, and arrested him under the Fugitive Offenders Act, 1881, on the following charges:

(a) Waging war or abetting the waging of war against His Majesty the King Emperor of India.

(b) Conspiring to deprive His Majesty the King of the sovereignty of British India or a part of it.

(c) Procuring and distributing arms and abetting the murder of Jackson.

(d) Procuring and distributing arms in London and waging war from London.

(e) Delivering seditious speeches in India from January to March, 1906 and in London from 1908 to 1909.

Unmindful of the Bow Street trickery perpetrated on him, Savarkar spent the night in the police lock-up and slept soundly because he had withstood the test of facing adversity. But his followers in London were upset by the manner in which he had been arrested. His comrade Aiyar took upon himself the task of arranging his defence and release.

On the morning of March 14, Savarkar was produced in the Bow Street Police Court. In the hearing that followed, application for his bail was moved by Reginald Vaughan. The Magistrate said that he needed to know more about the case before he could consider the request for his bail. So the bail was refused. He was remanded to custody for a week and on March 20, he was sent to Brixton Jail.

The evidence that was produced in the court later indicates that case against Savarkar was the result of the political intrigue of the British that originated from India. A telegram had been sent by the Viceroy of India to India Office in London stating that the "Government is anxious to proceed against Savarkar. His brother Ganesh has been convicted under Section 121 IPC. We agree that this is desirable and propose to send to London an Indian Police Officer having intimate knowledge of the Conspiracy Case here. We are advised that best evidence against Savarkar will be obtained from Sikhs and therefore have selected Sikh Deputy Superintendent Dyal Singh Gyani .... We request your sanction by telegraph to his deputation on these terms."

Since the well-wishers of Savarkar in London did not have the remotest idea of the scheming that was going on in the higher rungs of the political machinery in India, they believed that Savarkar would get a fair trial. Aiyar expressed this in a letter to Krishnavarma: "A solicitor was appointed and he conducted the case yesterday. He told me that if proper counsel was appointed, the trial can be made to take place here when, of course, his innocence can be established beyond a shadow of doubt." This hope largely rested on his being tried in England. That is why Aiyar also wrote that "We must do our best to see that he is not sent to India. If once he is sent, we shall see no more of him and one of the dearest and most devoted sons of the Motherland would be rotting away in the cells of a malarious island."

To realize their nefarious design, the authorities in India let the case drag on for months, by delaying the sending of papers related to it. This wore thin the patience and hope of the close associates of Savarkar. Aiyar, who visited him regularly, lost the zeal and also hope with which he had expressed the possibility of the positive outcome of the case to Krishnavarma. Now he felt sad that Savarkar had left Paris for England; he felt certain that he would either be put on gallows or be sent to the Andamans.

The sentiments of Aiyar reflected his respect for Savarkar and his contribution in organizing resistance against the British, but Savarkar had no feelings of regret that he had left the safety of Paris. He knew there was risk involved in that move, but he was willing to face its consequences. His spirits were high and his resolve firm as ever. It is in this spirit that he wrote his famous "My Will and Testament" to his sister-in-law Yasu Varini.

Written in a reminiscent mood, it recalls the happy days that they had shared and the path they had chosen to follow and the oaths they had taken to sacrifice their lives for their country.

In his "Will and Testament," he happily recalls the nature of the fight against the British and his readiness to sacrifice his life for the sacred cause: "The Test has come, O Ye! Who have taken the stern vows and pledged your solemn words to see the great sacrifice accomplished: Who is, say, ready to fall the first victim and immolate himself in this roaring fire that Good may triumph over the forces of Evil!"

Casting his fight in the mould of a holy fight for the sake of his Mother, in which all his brothers were involved, he tells her that he too is bound to **"Thy sacrificial Pillar! What of These! Had we been seven instead of only three I would have sacrificed them all—in thy cause."**

The cause is a Holy cause. "Thy Cause I believed to be the Cause of God! And in serving it I knew I served the Lord!"

"Thirty crores are Her Children! Those amongst them who possessed of this divine die in Her Cause shall ever live! And our family tree, O sister! thus uprooted shall strike its roots deep and bloom immortality."

Visualizing his impending sentence, which seemed almost certain, he writes: "We will work and die in defence

of Righteousness—thus had we pledged our words. Behold, we enter the flames! We have kept our word!"

"The stern vows we took to fight under Her banner in order to win Her Freedom back even at the cost of our lives have thus been fulfilled. What a relief! Blessed indeed are we that He should have given us strength to burn down the Self in us to ashes before our very eyes. We have served the Cause and fighting fell. This was all we aimed at!"

He speaks of his brother's valour and of his own resolve and urges his sister-in-law to believe and help in making his wife understand that "it was certainly not blindness that goaded us on to this Path! No! We entered on it under the full blaze of the searching light of Logic and History and Human Nature: knowing full well that Pilgrim's Progress leads through the valley of Death, we took up our Cross and deliberately followed Him."

These words not only testify to his resolve and commitment, but also show that the path chosen by him for the liberation of his country was chosen with full awareness of the risks that it involved.

When the papers for trying Savarkar finally arrived from India, it became quite clear why the authorities had taken that long to send them. They had made a strong case against him by resorting to treachery. They had roped in one Indian to testify against him and another one to speak lies that could be used against him. The Indian officials had seen to it that there was no need to seek evidence against Savarkar in London, for they wanted to ensure that he should be brought to India to face trial and get punished. That was the only way in which they could silence the revolutionary voice that had caused so much anxiety to the British.

Among the papers was the deposition of Harishchandra Koreagonkar who had been an active member of the Free Indian Society in India House during 1908-09. He had made a long statement, running into more than 120 typed pages, in which he had detailed all the activities that took place there, most of which were of a secret nature. More damagingly, he had stated that Savarkar and Aiyar were mainly responsible for whatever happened there; they were also responsible for instigating young people to take to the path of violence for liberating their motherland.

In their eagerness to prepare a foolproof case, the authorities did not leave anything to chance. They succeeded in making Chencheri Rama Rao, who had come from Burma to study in London and stayed at India House, agree to lie that the revolvers found in his box, for which he was in jail, were put in them by Savarkar. For agreeing to make that false statement, he earned his pardon and a lucrative job in the Police Department. This helped the authorities to show that the pistol that had been used to kill Jackson, the Mayor of Nasik, had been sent by Savarkar.

The police in India had thus evidence to prove that Savarkar was involved in waging war against the king as well as in the murder of Jackson.

The case opened on April 23, 1910 and charges against Savarkar were read out. In spite of his best efforts to plead that Savarkar be tried in England, Vaughan failed. The Magistrate at the Bow Street Police Court gave his decision on May 12 that Savarkar be sent to India to face trial there. Vaughan's application for a Writ of *Habeas Corpus* in the Divisional Court made on June 2 and 3, 1910 against the decision was also rejected.

A further appeal before the Court of Appeal too did not yield anything, for the majority of judges upheld the decision of sending Savarkar to India. The dissenting voice of Justice Coleridge was waived as a minority view.

In this way, Savarkar's trial in London was only meant to create the right kind of platform for his trial in India, in Nasik. That there was a dissenting voice amongst the judges against the decision to send him to India suggests that a neatly calculated conspiracy laden with vindictive motives was at work behind Savarkar's trial in London.

❑

Chapter 3

Nasik Conspiracy Case

While Savarkar was waiting for his trial in London, the colonial machinery in India was busy manufacturing and sending evidence against him to the British authorities to make sure that he was not sentenced there but sent to face another trial in India. In anticipation of that, the officials in India made full preparations to ensure that the trial within India produced the desired result of getting him sentenced for life and sending him away from the country, and thus put an end to the threat posed by him.

The efforts that the British government was making in India make it quite clear that it did not want Savarkar to stay free. The government feared that he would give a new orientation to the struggle for Indian independence. The political future of India would also have taken a different course.

As a significant part of their preparation for the anticipated trial of Savarkar, the British government in India promulgated a Special Ordinance to set up a Special Tribunal for his trial. It was truly special, because it was made in contravention of all the accepted norms of a proper judicial trial. For it provided neither for a jury nor any mechanism for making an appeal against the findings of the Tribunal. So the Tribunal had absolute power to do whatever it wanted. Since it looked like a body created mainly to punish rather than to try a person, it quite obviously negated the possibility of a free and fair trial.

That it was designed as a trap to ensnare Savarkar, to make certain that he is either sent to gallows or to the Andamans as a prisoner was sensed by fair-minded people even while he was in England. In response to his extradition to India, Guy Aldred drew the attention of the British public to the fact that all the courts involved in the trial of Savarkar in London "Bow Street Police Court, the Divisional Court and the Court of Appeal were characterized by the usual illegality. The English Government had determined on Savarkar's return to India." If this was what happened in England, one could easily guess what would happen in India, where the judicial system was always geared to serve the interests of the British. Lala Hardayal aptly stated that in India his "trial will only be a farce."

Given the concocted nature of the case and the determination of the British to get Savarkar sentenced in India, his friends resorted to desperate means to prevent his transportation to India. For this they made different kinds of plans.

One such plan truly bordered on the fantastic. It involved finding somebody who would have a close resemblance with Savarkar and sending him into his cell where he would exchange his place with him, and help the prisoner Savarkar walk out from the prison as a free man. This was too romantic and more like the stuff of fiction than something that could work. So it was not even tried.

Another plan was more realistic and workable, and it was tried. It envisaged to waylay the police van that carried Savarkar to and fro from his prison to the court at some convenient place and rescue him by using all possible means. Accordingly, on one particular day, when the police van was on its way to the court, it was ambushed and made to stop, but, to the disappointment of the people involved in planning the escape, there was no prisoner in it. Obviously, the plan had leaked and the police had ensured that the attempt met with failure.

Both these plans find a detailed mention in David Garnett's autobiography *The Golden Echo.*

On June 29, 1910 the then Secretary of State Winston Churchill issued orders that Savarkar be moved out of England and arrangements for his speedy transportation to India be put in place.

A letter was sent to the French government to inform them that an important political prisoner was to travel by P&O Liner S S Morea for India, obviously to scuttle any attempt by the Indian revolutionaries in Paris to help him in escaping from the ship.

The government also ordered the arrest of Aiyar, his close friend, to make sure that he did not do anything to create hurdles in the safe passage of Savarkar. But before the government could act, Aiyar had already planned his escape.

Aiyar put on the disguise of a Sikh and took a ship to Amsterdam. When a detective spotted him on the ship, he felt that he looked like Aiyar, but could not decide what to do till he saw VVS written on his suitcase. Feeling almost certain that he had found his man, he started questioning him. Aiyar promptly said to him that he had nothing to do with the person he was looking for, because he was Vir Vikram Singh.

After landing safely in Amsterdam, Aiyar took a train to Paris and joined Krishnavarma and Madam Cama to prepare for a meeting with Savarkar at the port of Marseilles.

Meanwhile S S Morea set sail from England on July 1, 1910. It was scheduled to make a stop at Marseilles because it had to collect mail and some passengers, too. When Savarkar came to know about this, he envisioned in this an opportunity of his escape, though he was not sure if his fellow-revolutionaries in Europe had any plan for his rescue. On the dawn of July 8, he told his two guards that he needed to go to the water closet. Once inside, he took off his nightgown to cover the glass pane to prevent them from watching what he was doing inside. Then he squeezed himself out of the pothole and jumped into the sea.

When the guards saw this, they raised alarm, but Savarkar managed to escape unharmed and reached the shore. Then he climbed the quay. He cried out of joy because he was sure that he was on free land, where the British could not even touch him.

Unfortunately, his joy proved short-lived. On the road, he shouted for the French police, to take him to the nearest police station, but they did not oblige. He moved away from the scene to escape the British police that was in his pursuit. He could not hire a cab, because he had no money. Seeing that he was running and shouting, and the British police were running after him and shouting "Thief! Thief! Catch him," the French police caught him, and handed him over to the British police, who dragged him back to the ship.

This episode was truly unfortunate. Though Savarkar's revolutionary friends in Paris had framed a rescue plan, they could not reach the port in time to save him. Savarkar did not expect the French police to act irresponsibly by handing him over to the British police, because it was a clear violation of International Law. Nevertheless, Savarkar's unsuccessful attempt was noticed the world over and its echoes reverberated for a long while, and became the basis of another trial, called The Hague trial.

The British police arrested Savarkar on the French soil, even though they had no jurisdiction over him. They did not want to lose their prize prisoner at any cost. They, in fact, had been preparing for months to get rid of the menace that had put them on tenterhooks. They had alerted the French police in advance, and they helped in restoring him to them.

The incident was widely reported in the French press and almost everybody called it an international scandal and a violation of the right of asylum. Savarkar's friends in France approached the French government to take serious note of the violation committed by Britain and demanded that he be returned to France. M Jaures, the grandson of Karl Marx and the Mayor of Marseilles, initiated the move in this regard.

The President of the League of Man's Rights who was approached by Ranaji also wrote a letter to the French Minister of Foreign Affairs that Savarkar be returned to France, failing which the matter would be referred to the Hague Court of Arbitration.

The response of the French government came on July 19: "The French government, in view of the fact that Savarkar actually landed on the French soil, have requested the British government to suspend the trial, till full reports on the case are received."

The French press condemned its police for violating the rights of a fugitive seeking asylum. In England, Guy Aldred formed the "Release Savarkar Committee" and conducted a full-scale campaign for his release. Embassies from all over the world raised their voice against the action of the French police. As a consequence of this, the French government was compelled to make a demand for the return of Savarkar to France. The result was that a new trial had to be arranged at The Hague to go into the case, which will be dealt with in a separate chapter. It was also reported later that the French policeman who had handed over Savarkar to the British police was sent to jail for dereliction of duty.

Meanwhile, after getting him back from the French soil, Savarkar's guards brought him to the ship and put him in chains. When the ship reached Aden, he was transferred to another steamer SS Sasti, amidst tight security. His guards shut him in a tiny cabin, where he could neither move nor walk, only stand. He had no access to sunlight. But he braved it all with fortitude.

SS Sasti landed in Bombay on July 22, 1910 . Savarkar came out handcuffed and had to march through rows of drawn swords. Then he was driven out in a closed van and transferred to a well-guarded train, which took him to the Nasik Police custody. After some days, he was put in the Yervada Jail in Poona.

Savarkar's trial got mired in controversy, because the question of his extradition had to be settled before it could be started. This led to a furious exchange of cables between the Governor's office in Bombay and the India Office in London. The Governor in Bombay was keen that there should be no delay in starting the trial. This is clear from the fact that he threatened to resign, if he was not allowed to start the proceedings. He did not want that the effort of making and breaking witnesses in India to make an iron clad case against Savarkar should get wasted.

The man in charge of affairs in London Lord Morley, who had not yet given his consent to proceed in the matter, had to leave his post to take over as the Lord President of the Council. The new incumbent did not take much time to permit the Governor to start the trial, stating that if international commitments demanded that Savarkar be restored to France after the announcement of judgment, then that would be done. That is how the Nasik trial, an offshoot of the trial in London, started in India.

Joseph Baptista, a well-known lawyer, came from Paris at Madame Cama's behest, to plead for Savarkar. The administrative machinery in Bombay had already done its job to perfection. A special Tribunal, as we have mentioned, was already in place. It consisted of Basil Scott, the Chief Justice of Bombay, N G Chandavarkar and Justice Heaton. The counsel for prosecution consisted of the Advocate General of Bombay Jardine, Seldon, Welinkar, and Nicolson, the public prosecutor. Savarkar was represented by Jospeh Bapista, Govindrao Gadgil, Chtire, and Rangnekar.

In Nasik, Savarkar was tried in three cases. In the first one, there were thirty-eight accused and Savarkar. In the second one, there were only two: Gopalrao Patankar and Savarkar. In the third one, Savarkar was the sole accused.

In all, there were eight charges against him, for which the government had already set up four approvers: Kashinath Ankushkar, Dattatray Joshi, W R Kukarni, and Chaturbuj Amin, who worked as a cook in India House, through whom Savarkar was alleged to have sent twenty pistols to India.

For conducting the trial, Savarkar was shifted from Yervada Jail to Dongri Jail. When he was brought in a closed car to the High Court with an armed escort, he was told to enter the dock of prisoners. When he entered the place, all the accused welcomed him with a standing ovation. Many of them were there only because, in one way or the other, they had taken part in his activities, and yet they cheered him. When he was offered a chair to sit by the side of the advocates, as a special concession, he declined, and chose to stay with the prisoners. As expected, nobody from among the people was permitted to witness the proceedings; the galleries were empty.

The trial was opened by Jardine, the main prosecution counsel, and he spoke for the whole day. When the court opened again after ten days, on September 26, 1910, the defence counsel argued that the Tribunal should stay the proceedings to allow Savarkar to appeal against his arrest on the French soil, but the objection was overruled.

Jardine presented his arguments again for two more days, on September 27 and 28. Prosecution witnesses were examined and cross-examined. Savarkar was given the option to cross-examine them, but he refused to do that. He pleaded that he did not recognize the jurisdiction of the Tribunal to try him, because he was entitled to the right of asylum in France and the protection of French law. He also said that he had abandoned himself to the mercy of the French nation, which called itself the land of fraternity, equality and liberty. He refused to take any further part in the trial, because he called it illegal. Savarkar's counsel Baptista too argued that the arrest of Savarkar was illegal.

As expected, the objections of Savarkar and his counsel were overruled. But on October 1, some provisions of the Extradition Act were discussed in the court. Savarkar too was questioned in this regard, but he held on to his earlier position and did not respond to anything. Finally, the court held that even if his arrest at Marseilles was illegal, "it did not affect the powers of the Indian Law Court to try him."

Meanwhile, as the trial continued, people inside and outside India expressed their concern about the outcome of the trial and the safety of Savarkar. Shyamji Krishnavarma expressed his deep anxiety over the two issues to Rambhau Mandlik, who, as the editor of *Vihari,* had already voiced his concern about Savakar's health and safety. Krishnavarma wrote to him to say:

> I am sorry to say that my knowledge of the crooked ways of the Indian police does not allow me to be equally sanguine. There is no knowing where the Indian police might stop when they have set their hearts upon doing a certain thing. By hook or by crook, they will carry out their objective...
>
> I am unfortunately cognizant also with many instances of police monstrosities which all make me much afraid of Mr Savarkar's safety in the hands of Nasik CID at the present moment. A recent telegram from India says that some 48 new arrests have been made in connection with the Nasik Conspiracy Case. This development has taken place after Mr Savarkar being placed in the hands of Indian police.

As the trial proceeded, the prosecution withdrew the charge that Savarkar had waged war against the King, which ended the second trial even before it could start.

In all, more than three hundred witnesses were examined and cross-examined. Most of them admitted openly that they were compelled to give evidence against the accused, because they were threatened. A large number of documents were also exhibited. After that, the Chief Justice, once again, asked Savarkar if he had to say anything in his defence, to which he said "No." He only made the following comment:

> I am quite innocent of the charges made against me. I took part in the proceedings of the trial in England where courts are established by democratic rules sanctioned by the people. In such courts, one can expect to get justice. There the authority does not rely upon brute force. The condition of Indian courts of law is quite the reverse. I am not amenable to the jurisdiction of the Indian courts of law. I, therefore, decline to give any statement or bring any evidence for my defence.

Since Savarkar held on to this view, the defence too concentrated on arguing the illegality of the trial. This prompted another long response from the Attorney General that lasted nearly a week. Savarkar bore all of that with calm and even helped to restore the sagging morale of the other accused and the defence lawyers. Considering the manner in which the trial had proceeded, Savarkar knew what the outcome would be. To make sure that it did not spread despondency among the accused, he thought it appropriate to tell them that whatever was happening was for the sake of their Motherland, to whom they all owed a debt.

After nearly ten weeks of efforts put in by the lawyers on both sides in which scores of witnesses were examined and re-examined, the verdict was finally announced on December 23, 1910. Savarkar's name was on top of the list of the convicted and the verdict was: "transportation for life and forfeiture of all your property."

The judgment against Savarkar was fairly long, because it provided a detailed account of almost all his activities, related to the cause of India's freedom, right from the time of his school days to the time of his stay in London. These were meant to establish an uninterrupted chain of his numerous activities that were meant to initiate and support "revolutionary conspiracy," directed towards political assassinations with pistols and other explosive devices. These conspiracies were traced to numerous cities, such as Nasik, Bombay, Yeola, Aurangabad and other places in the Deccan and directed by the energy of Savarkar.

In some respects, the judgment is an important document, because it provides details about the activities of Savarkar that show his love for his country in full measure. We learn how he formed the *Mitra Mela*, a strong group of young people, during early days in India, and undertook to educate the public through lectures, books and songs and to prepare them to fight the British with arms. This small organization eventually became *Abhinava Bharat*, the Young India Society, which was modelled on the revolutionary societies in Italy.

The judgment makes special mention of Savarkar's *Life of Mazzini*, translated by him into Marathi, as an inspirational work, for "elevating politics to the rank of religion and argues that Ramdas, the saint of Maharashtra in the time of Shivaji, possessed the same spiritual essence as Mazzini under a different name. It points out how Mazzini relied upon the youth of the country to attain independence and then proceeds to dilate upon his twofold programme of instruction and war."

Another interesting feature of the judgment is that it helps to clarify certain ideas and their association with Savarkar for which the nationalist historians of India have not given him any credit. For example, it mentions his concept of *Swadeshi* agitation, by which is "meant the imposition of restraint upon the plundering propensities of another and the protection of one's own interests. The boycott of foreign goods should lead to the boycott of the foreigners." This Savarkar said and practiced several decades before it become the propaganda plank of the Indian National Congress, for which credit has always been given to Gandhi.

The judgment also provides a picture of the activities that Savarkar organized in London during his stay there. These include his writings and speeches, his inspirational pamphlets that he sent to India, and his appeal to the Indian princes to choose their options wisely.

The decision that went against Savarkar was *ex parte* and arbitrary because it rested on the uncontested evidence of the prosecution. The Tribunal did not even recognize the illegality of Savarkar's arrest as it was *sub judice* in the International Court of Arbitration at The Hague.

The scene after the announcement of the judgement was worth watching. Slogans raised by the accused *"Vande Matram"* and *"Bharat Mata Ki Jai"* echoed around the place. The people who had gathered outside joined the chorus of the accused. The police could not stop this show of patriotic fervour. But they did stop Savarkar from coming out of the dock and bidding farewell to his brother.

The dread in which the Indian government, led by Lord Sydenham, held Savarkar can also be seen in what followed after the judgment was delivered. It instituted another case against him, charging him with abetment of the murder of the Collector of Nasik. The very same Tribunal was asked to try him, once again. The illegality was thus compounded.

Even in this trial, which was only meant to ensure that he should not return to India after completing his term of life-imprisonment of twenty-five years, Savarkar held on to his stand and refused to take part in the proceedings. He did not want that his case should get prejudiced at the International Court.

The trial opened on January 23, 1911. The Advocate General summed up the case against Savarkar. After that, he was called to make his say. As expected, Savarkar said that he was innocent and he had no direct or indirect connection with the murder of Jackson. The only piece of evidence against him was the pamphlet *Vande Matram,* which had been found with Chengiri Rao. Besides, it was sent from London many days after the murder had taken place. He also denied that the pistol that was used for killing Jackson had been sent by him.

Whatever Savarkar said in his defence had no effect on the Tribunal. This was even expected, for its job was only to complete the due process of prosecution so that they could announce their decision. Unabashedly, the Tribunal slapped a second transportation for life on Savarkar.

The response of Savarkar to the pronouncement of the Tribunal is worthy of attention. He rose up and said:

> I am prepared to face ungrudgingly the extreme penalty of your laws, in the belief that it is through sufferings and sacrifice alone that out beloved Motherland can march to an assured, if not a speedy triumph.

The response to two transportations in one life was wittier:

> I must thank you, My Lord—for at least one thing. That, by proclaiming "two life transportations to one" you have confirmed the Hindu belief of "Life after Life" and the theory of reincarnation. (*punarjanma*)

The sentence was obviously unique and unheard of. Fearing adverse publicity for its unjust dispensation, the British government made sure that judgments of both these trials were not put in the Law Reports. The newspapers too avoided publishing them.

After the verdict was announced, Savarkar was handcuffed and removed from the scene by an armed guard. He had a Marathi song on his lips:

Pleased be thou, mother! To acknowledge this little service of thy children. Boundless is our indebtedness to thee! Thou chose us to bless and suckle us at thy breast!

Behold! We enter the flames of this consecrated Fire today. The first instalment of that debt of Love we pay.

And totally taking a new birth there and then will we immolate ourselves over and over again till the hungry God of sacrifice be full and crown Thee with glory.

With Shree Krishna for Thy redoubtable charioteer, and Shree Ram to lead and thirty crores of soldiers to fight under thy banner,

The army stops not though we fall!

But pressing on shall utterly rout the forces of Evil and Thy right hand, Oh Mother, shall plant the golden Banner of Righteousness and Independence on the Triumphant Tops of the Himalayas.

Then Savarkar was shifted from the Dongri Jail, where he had been kept during the trial, to the Byculla Jail and from there he was taken to Thane. From there he was transported to the Andamans, where he was lodged in jail on July 3, 1911. He was put in a solitary cell and brought to India in 1921, put again in Yervada Jail, and released conditionally in 1924.

Week long centenary celebrations of the event were held from July 3 to July 9 in 2011, both in and outside the jail. Thousands of Savarkar admirers flew from all corners of the world to attend the celebrations and pay homage to him. The author was specially invited and honoured on the occasion, and he spoke on both days.

❑

Chapter 4
The Hague Trial

When Savarkar escaped from SS Morea, swam towards the French shore, and succeeded in planting his feet on the French soil, he thought he had escaped from the clutches of the British government and was a free man. Sadly, things did not turn out that way. With the help of a French policeman, the British police that was running after him, took control of him, and brought him back to his cell in the ship.

Because he was taken back to the ship from the French soil, the incident invited worldwide attention; both the general public as well as experts from several countries felt that it involved a breach of International Law, a violation of the right to asylum. The result was that the French government came under severe pressure to ask the British government to return Savarkar to them.

On the 4th and 5th of October, 1910, the governments of England and France exchanged notes on this issue. But instead of sorting it out between themselves, they decided to submit to arbitration the questions of fact and law raised by the arrest of Savarkar on the French soil and the demand of the French Republic for his restitution to them.

The two governments signed an Agreement on October 25, 1910 to constitute the Arbitral Tribunal, the questions to be submitted to it, and the procedures to be followed, on the basis of the following Articles.

Article 1 stated the question to be decided: Should Savarkar, in conformity with the rules of international law, be restored by the British government to the French Republic?

Article 2 provided that the Tribunal shall be constituted of five arbitrators chosen from the members of the Permanent Court at The Hague. Together, the two governments would decide on its composition and have the freedom to choose one arbitrator from among their nationals.

Article 3 stated that on December 6, 1910, each of the parties would forward to the Bureau of the Permanent Court fifteen copies of its case, with duly certified copies of documents that it wanted, and the Bureau would forward them to the arbitrators and to each party: three copies to the arbitrators and two to each party. Two copies would remain in the archives of the Bureau. It further stated that the contracting parties would deposit their counter-cases with supporting documents in the same manner. Since these might necessitate replies, these were to be presented within fifteen days after the delivery of the counter-cases. However, the dates for the presentation of cases, counter-cases, and replies could be extended by mutual agreement between the two parties.

Article 4 fixed the meeting of the Tribunal at The Hague: February 14, 1911. Each party was to be represented by an Agent, who would serve as an intermediary between the governments and the Tribunal. The Court could ask the Agent to provide oral or written explanations, to which the Agent of the other party had the right to reply.

Article 5 allowed the parties as well as the members of the Tribunal to use either the English or French language for their deliberations; the decisions of the Tribunal would, however, be drawn in both the languages.

Article 6 stated that the award of the Tribunal would be given as soon as possible, but within 30 days following the date of its meeting at The Hague or the delivery of the explanations that might have been furnished. This period could be extended on the request of the Tribunal, if the two parties agreed to this.

The two governments also agreed that in case questions arise in the course of the arbitration that are not covered by the terms of the Agreement, these shall be determined by the provisions of the International Convention for the Pacific Settlement of International Disputes signed at The Hague on 18th October, 1907.

The two governments had to bear expenses for attending to the arbitration process on their own and also an equal share of expenses of the Tribunal.

The questions for the Tribunal related to:

(a) Facts related to the case.

(b) Matters related to international law.

The Tribunal needed to know the facts so that it could interpret them, and then apply the appropriate principles of international law to decide on the question relating to Savarkar's restitution by England to France.

The facts related to the circumstances in which Savarkar was arrested in England to the time he was taken back from the French soil to the ship in which he was to travel to India. These were presented by both the governments in their respective cases and counter-cases along with their implications related to the vital question of the violation of international law.

The facts of the case in brief are:

Savarkar was arrested in London on several charges on March 13, 1910. A magisterial inquiry was conducted by Albert de Rutzen to ascertain whether Savarkar ought to be returned to India for trial. After considering written evidence transmitted from India as per The Fugitive Offenders Act, 1881 and also on the oral evidence presented there, the Magistrate ordered that he be sent to India to face trial. Though Savarkar used all possible legal means permitted within the law of England, the Courts that heard his appeal against the decision held that the order of the Magistrate was "regular and lawful."

On June 29, 1910, after the completion of all the required legal proceedings, the Secretary of State for Home Affairs, Winston Churchill, issued the warrant of Savarkar's return to India, and appointed Charles John Power, Deputy Superintendent of the Bombay Provincial Police to take Savarkar into custody and convey him to India.

On July 1, Savarkar left on board SS Morea, under the supervision of John Power, for Marseilles, where she had to collect mail and passengers. Inspector Parker of the London Criminal Investigation Department, who was to give witness at Savarkar's trial in India, and two Indian constables who worked directly under John Power to guard him, were part of the police team.

On June 29, Sir E Henry, the Chief Commissioner of Police of London, wrote to the Chief of the French Police M Hennion to inform him that Savarkar was being sent to India by the Morea and requested him to ensure his safety while the ship was in the port because of the possibility of interference with the escort of Savarkar by Indian extremists. Hennion sent his reply on July 9, in which he stated that he had given necessary instructions in that regard. Before sending this reply, he had already sent a message to the concerned officers in France.

On July 7, when the ship arrived at Marseilles, the Commissaire Special of the port, M Leblais, came on board the ship. Parker introduced him to John Power and also pointed Savarkar to him. On the way to his cabin, the Commissaire showed to Inspector Parker the letter relating to the assistance to be given by the French police to the officers in charge of Savarkar. He then took Parker out to introduce him to the French policemen. All this happened before the incident of Savarkar's escape from the ship.

Although there could be a possibility of divergent perceptions of the happening that took place on July 8, there was no substantial difference between the British and French versions about what happened after this.

At about 6.30 a.m. Savarkar was under the charge of the two Indian constables. He asked for going to the W.C., bolted the door from inside, covered the glass with his gown, sought the pothole, squeezed himself, jumped into the sea, and swam to the quay. Since the two constables could not enter the W.C., they raised their voice to draw the attention of the French police that was already there to guard the ship.

Savarkar had covered about three hundred yards of the French soil, when one of the French officers took hold of him, and brought him back to the ship. The role of the ship's steward and the two constables was only to assist the French officer. After that the ship left the port for Aden, where Savarkar was transferred into another ship.

The British government received communication from the French government about the incident at Marseilles on July 18, only after the ship had left Aden. The French Ambassador in Britain, M Cambon, communicated to Sir Edward Grey, the Secretary of State for Foreign Affairs, a note informing that the French Minister of Foreign Affairs had been informed about the incident and suggested that Savarkar, having acquired the right to asylum, had been handed over to the British police by mistake; therefore, he be returned. But the British government refused to comply.

Considering the facts of the case, and the terms agreed by the two governments, the Arbitration Tribunal was set up. The very composition of the Tribunal shows that it was meant to produce a pre-conceived result. Strong nations like Germany and Russia did not figure in it. Instead, its members were Belgium's former Prime Minister, M Beernaert, Norway's former minister, MG Gram, Holland's member of the Second Chamber, Jonkheer Lohman, England's Earl of Desart, and France's Louis Renault. The British agent was Eyre A Crowe, of the Foreign Office, who was assisted by Joseph Addison. The French agent was M Andre Weiss, jurisconsult adjoint of the Ministry of Foreign Affairs, who was assisted by M Camille Jordan. The Secretary General of the Tribunal was Baron Michiels Van Verduynen, Secretary of the Permanent Court of Arbitration.

The trial opened on February 16, 1911 and though expected to last for about a month, as per Article 6, the Tribunal completed its work after a few hurried meetings, and gave its judgment in favour of the British government, to which we will come later.

On the basis of the inquiries that the French Government made about the incident, they advanced three propositions:

(a) That Savarkar on reaching French soil had acquired a *"droit d'asile."*

(b) That the British officers violated the sovereignty of France by taking active part in the arrest of Savarkar on the French soil.

(c) That Savarkar was handed over to the British authorities by a subordinate official in error; his act was irregular according to the French municipal law and the international law.

So the French government demanded that he be handed back to the French authorities.

The British put forth their case in response to the three propositions one by one. About the first one, they maintained that no foreigner can have a *"droit dasile"* in which it has sought refuge. On the basis of certain known cases, it stated that the question of surrender depends on the will of the State of refuge, and not on any right vested in the refugee. In fact, the issue does not fall within the domain of international law but of constitutional controversies. As such, the contention of the French Republic is not founded on any principle of international law.

As to the question of violation of French sovereignty by the British police, it was maintained that every state has a right to refuse hospitality to an alien, or determine the conditions or terms on which any alien is allowed to enter its territory. The French government had already committed themselves to protecting Savarkar and ensuring that he be not allowed to come ashore on his own or with the assistance of Indian extremists. The French officer who saw Savarkar escape gave him chase and recaptured him only because of the instructions that had been given to him and other French officers.

The ship's steward and the Indian constables did not offer any affront to the sovereignty of France, because all that they did was to raise an outcry when Savarkar escaped and followed the French officer in pursuit. The French officer had already caught hold of him, and was in his custody when the Indian policemen joined him and held one of his arms. As such, it did not in any way constitute any assertion of British authority in France. The policemen did not arrest Savarkar all by themselves, nor did they oppose the French officer in whatever he was doing; they only gave assistance to him.

Even if the movement of the British policemen on the French soil is seen as going beyond ordinary assistance to a competent officer of the law, it was given in perfect good faith and also in accordance with mutual understanding and trust. Therefore, there is no reason to believe that there was any kind of violation, direct or indirect, on the part of the British policemen of the French sovereignty.

With regard to the issue of the error made by the French official by handing over Savarkar to the British police, the British maintained that the French have not specified the nature of the error committed by him: was he in error as to the identity of Savarkar or the fact of his escape?

The fact is that the officer had already been instructed to ensure that there was no interference from any quarter with regard to the detention of Savarkar. When he saw what was happening and heard shouts of the policemen, he was right in inferring that the occasion had arisen when he should act without waiting for any special instruction from the British officials. All that passed between him and Savarkar was his reply to his question when he asked him if he was a French policeman. He did not speak anything to the policemen. Therefore, there was no error on the part of the French official with regard to the identity of Savarkar.

The only other question that needed to be addressed is whether the French official (Brigadier Pasquie) had exceeded his powers and duties under the municipal law of France or the international law.

The French Republic had not provided any information about the French municipal law to invalidate the action of the official. With regard to the violation of the international law, it is quite clear that the officer acted in accordance with the understanding that had already been set forth between the two governments about the prisoner. He did his duty, acted in good faith, and obviously did not violate any international law.

Two examples from the past were quoted in support of the view that since no violation of any kind had taken place, the British government was under no obligation to return Savarkar to the French Republic.

The Tribunal did not find many divergences between the cases of the two governments. The French case, in fact, supplemented the British case, by providing more details about the correspondence between the two governments.

In response to this, the French not only reiterated their position, but also clarified their stand on the nature of the error of Brigadier Pasquie. The Brigadier had informed his superiors on July 23 that he did not know that the fugitive he had helped to restore to the British was Savarkar. So the French case rested mainly now on this error. Because of this, Savarkar became the victim of irregular extradition.

In response to this, the British argument was that the identity of the person surrendered might raise questions in a municipal court, but has no significance in this case of arbitration.

Besides, the British argued that it was difficult to believe that the Brigadier did not know the identity of the prisoner. He had already said that he saw Savarkar come out of the porthole, he himself pursued and caught him, and could not speak with the policemen because of the language barrier.

Inspector Parker considered the statement of the Brigadier incomplete. He said that the officer went down with Parker and the steward and the constables to the deck and to the cabin in which Savarkar had been confined before his escape. While below, Parker saw him and spoke with him in French, but he did not make any inquiry about the prisoner. If he had, he would have been told at once who Savarkar was and what share he had in Hindu revolutionary projects.

It was further argued that if the declaration made by Brigadier Pasquie is examined carefully, it becomes quite clear that he did not regard the man arrested by him as an ordinary seaman deserter who had been carrying on his duties as the crew on board. The Brigadier himself says that the persons who followed Savarkar were charged with his surveillance.

In that case, it is quite easily seen that the person arrested by him is no ordinary marine deserter who takes advantage of the presence of his ship in port and who runs towards the shore. A man under surveillance can only be a person who is guilty of having committed some crime; he is not a mere deserter but an escaping prisoner.

Further, it seems reasonable to assume that the Brigadier would have talked about the incident to his superior officers, including Commissaire Leblais, who knew who Savarkar was. When Leblais came down in the afternoon, twenty hours before the ship left the port, he was shown how Savarkar had escaped and how he had been brought back. At that time, he did not make any protest, nor did he mention the ignorance of the Brigadier. He simply said that he had to make a report to his Administration about the incident.

Besides, the telegram of the Prefect of Marseilles suggests that up to the 13th of July no suggestion had reached him that the Brigadier had made any error of fact "which is said to vitiate his surrender of the prisoner."

At no time in the diplomatic correspondence between the two governments, and not till the presentation of the case did this suggestion even figure that the fugitive was a marine deserter or any other person. For such persons written requests are made by the master of the ship.

It also seems unfair to suggest that inspector Parker was guilty of accepting the return of Savarkar and that he deliberately refrained from telling the Brigadier about the identity of Savarkar. It is based on the assumption that he was ignorant about it, which seems unreasonable to assume because the Brigadier was one of the gendarmes who had been pointed out by Leblais as being in charge of the prisoner about whom special instructions had been issued.

Besides, at no point did the Brigadier suggest that he was "in any way deceived or misled by any act or omission on the part of Mr Parker."

The British held that the claim of the French Republic would be valid only if their government had acquired possession of Savarkar by a violent invasion of French territory or if they had induced France to hand him over to them by resorting to fraudulent means or falsehood. In that case the Tribunal could then direct the British to hand over Savarkar to them. But as the events had unfolded, and as they had been described by the French themselves, there was no violence and no fraud and no falsehood had been used. He was voluntarily given back to the British by a responsible officer of the police, and if he now claims that he was not clear about what he was supposed to do, that in no way obligates it to hand one of its own subjects back to the French government.

As things stand, in receiving Savarkar from the French authorities, there was no violation of any international law.

So the main task of the Tribunal, argued the British, was to ascertain the facts and circumstances of the case and rights and obligations under the international law.

It is interesting to note that Longuet, attorney in the Court of Appeal at Paris, too presented the case on behalf of Savarkar.

His plea rested on the belief that no principle of the Court precludes a private person to be heard or to make the defence of his interests. Though the case is principally between two countries, the Court stands to benefit to hear accurate statements of Savarkar as well as the testimonies of those who have been involved in the incidents causing the dispute. His arguments throw additional light on the nature of Savarkar's arrest on the French soil and its legal implications.

To put his plea in its proper perspective, the attorney reconstructed Savarkar's past, right form the time of his student days in India, focusing on his activities on the Indian soil, his move to London to study law and his connection with organizing political meetings there, and the case against him by the Gray's Inn.

The thrust of this presentation was to establish that Savarkar was a known political being and not a criminal. That is why when he went to Paris after the death of Jackson, and stayed on for four months, the British government did not make any request for his extradition; they knew their request would not be granted. The British also knew that he could be arrested only after he returned to London.

In London, he was charged with crimes committed by him in 1906 in India, because that was the only way in which he could be sent back to India.

The counsel dwelt on the incident at Marseilles, and held that when Morea was in the French territorial waters, the British had lost its jurisdiction, a fact that Savarkar, being a student of law, knew very well. He cited the case of the Mexican refugee Gomez in support of his contention.

Then he presented Savarkar's version about his arrest on the French soil, stating that he was caught by the British police and not by the French police.

Another version provided by the journalist Gabriel M Bellin is that he was caught by the police of both countries. He says that when they caught him, they perhaps did not think that they had done anything illegal; they were only doing their duty. It is apparent, he notes, that given the circumstances in which the arrest took place, Savarkar "should have been entrusted to a French magistrate, better informed about the thorny issues of international law than the police."

The British version, as is already known, is that he was arrested by the French and the British police took only his delivery.

The contention of Savarkar's counsel is that there is some problem with the British version, and this is clear from the fact that "the Indian police on the Morea have since themselves destroyed the interpretation of the facts in the official account they gave of the incidents wherein they strongly emphasize the part they played in the arrest of Savarkar."

Because of divergent views on the incident of Savarkar's arrest, the lawyer sent to Marseilles his own team of people, for on the spot investigation on 13, 14, and 15 January.

They found that the Brigadier's version was the same that he had given earlier. When Savarkar ran on the French soil, people were following him, shouting "thief." He too ran and caught him by his left arm. The British police, which was also in chase, caught him by his right arm and his neck.

The lawyer's argument was that even if Pasquie is to be believed, the vital question that needs to be addressed is: Did he have the jurisdiction and standing as a representative of the French state to do what he did? According to judicial precedents, which are available in law magazines and journals, Pasquie had the status of a local policeman, and nothing else.

Another noticeable thing in the matter is that the cries of "thief" were uttered by the police not only when they were chasing him, but also from the bridge of the boat; even the guards on the ship shouted "thief."

Because of this, argued the lawyer, the good faith of the French police officer was abused; he was made to believe that the fugitive was an offender or an ordinary criminal and not a revolutionary writer and a nationalist against whom "weighed only political charges. Only by the deception about the true nature of the prisoner, his assistance was obtained—assuming that his assistance had ever been effective and real."

So the lawyer stated that on the basis of all available evidence and no matter what version of Savarkar's arrest is believed, some conclusions can easily be drawn:

- The police arrested Savarkar on the French territory and forcibly returned him to the ship.
- The role of Pasquie in this was minimal, entirely secondary, for he acted only as an adjunct.
- By virtue of his assistance, it cannot engage in any degree the French authorities; he was acting merely as an executing agency.
- The contribution of Pasquie in the entire operation is flawed. Like the maritime police, he was misled about the true nature of the fugitive and also by the shouts of 'thief.'

It can be easily concluded that the reasons for Savarkar's arrest are irrefutable, for he was arrested arbitrarily and illegally, by fraud and error, snatched from the French soil and should be returned.

The lawyer quoted several legal authorities in support of his contention. Savarkar's trial in Nasik that started immediately after his arrival in India also proved that he was a political prisoner and therefore entitled to refuge in France.

The Tribunal, as already stated, gave its judgment in favour of the British, while admitting that an irregularity had been committed in the arrest of Savarkar and in his being handed over to the British police.

The judgment narrated the facts related to the case almost in the manner already described. On the basis of that the court held that "Whereas, having reacted to what has been stated, it is manifest that the case is not one of recourse to fraud or force in order to obtain possession of a person who had taken refuge in a foreign country, and that there was not in the circumstances of the arrest and delivery of Savarkar to the British authority and of his removal to India anything in the nature of the violation of the sovereignty of France, and that all those who took part in the matter certainly acted in good faith and had no thought of doing anything unlawful.

"Whereas, in the circumstances cited above, the conduct of the Brigadier, not having been disclaimed by his chiefs before the morning of July 9, i.e., before the Morea left Marseilles, the British police might naturally have believed that the Brigadier had acted in accordance with his instructions or that his conduct had been approved.

"Whereas, **while admitting that an irregularity was committed by the arrest of Savarkar and by his being handed over to the British police, there is no rule of International Law imposing, in circumstances such as those which have been set out above, any obligation on the power, which in its custody a prisoner, to restore him because of a mistake**

committed by the foreign agent who delivered him to that power."

It is quite obvious that the Tribunal accepted the agruments put forward by the British and decided the case in their favour, but to give it some respectability, it put in a qualifying phrase that "an irregularity had been committed," to lessen its shocking impact.

Since the judgment of the Tribunal was patently biased in favour of the British, it produced shock waves throughout the world. Legal authorities commented that it made a mockery of the established right of asylum as cited in International Law.

Hamelin in L'affairs Savarkar, defended the French view, but it was criticized in *Law Magazine and Review*, 36 (1911).

Shyamji Krishnavarma wrote in his *Indian Sociologist*:

> The decision of the International Tribunal has shattered all faith in the maintenance of the rights of political refugees as ordinarily understood and it is sad to observe that the nations, hitherto most conspicuous for their love of liberty, are slow to recognise these rights when they are beset by political considerations. L' Humanite was after all justified in finding that the submission of L'Affairs Savarkar to arbitration in the first instance was a tactical error on the part of France and a friend, who was a member of the British Parliament, assures us that the way in which France submitted her case ensured its failure, all the strongest grounds having been omitted.
>
> There only remains for us to offer an expression of our heartfelt sympathy and commiseration with our dear friend and associate, Mr Vinayak Damodar Savarkar in the hard fate that has befallen him, and which has snatched him from us at the very moment when ... we were all so confident of speedily seeing him once more in our midst. We also desire to tender our sincere

condolence to the members of his family, **who have had the agony of seeing three brothers one after another doomed to incarceration, two of them having been sentenced to transportation for life."**

This reaction from Krishnavarma is quite understandable. The two knew each other and were revolutionaries and comrades in arms.

In England, reactions to the decision of the Tribunal were sharper. The press, in fact, ridiculed the whole affair.

Dr Oppenheim, a known authority on International Law, commented on the case in *The Daily News*, in the following words: "The judgment reduces the right of asylum to very narrow limits. According to the judgment, to put the matter in its extreme form, a Prince called Kropotkin might conceivably be kidnapped by Russian agents in collusion with British police and without the knowledge or consent of the British Government and no rule of International Law could be invoked for his restoration.

"The decision emphasizes the urgent need for the establishment, as supplementary to the Arbitration Courts at The Hague of a permanent court of International Law, from which, not negative compromises, but sensible authoritative judgments could be obtained."

The Berlin Post, an organ of the Free Conservative Society was more scathing in its editorial comment:

> We have never thought much of The Hague Court of Arbitration—that is, of its impartiality and objective love of justice. The representatives of the various nationalities vote, in point of fact, in accordance with the interests, the political views, and the grounds of expediency, of their several countries—always excepting our idealist Germans. It is not necessary to suppose that these men act in the fact of their better judgment and conscience. To some extent foreign countries have a different, and certainly a much more practical, sense of values,

in striking a balance, as between the interests of their own country, and the conception of pure justice as it prevails in general with us. National prejudices and prepossessions determine the judgment from the outset.

Nevertheless, we should hardly have thought it possible that a court of arbitration in the Savarkar Case would accord an exhibition of such naivete, such an exhibition of pure folly. It has passed over the real issue of the Savarkar Case in complete silence—namely, the fact that a political offender, who is in a foreign harbour had escaped from the ship which was transporting him and been recaptured by a French policeman with the support of an Englishman in pursuit and that not in the water, though there already he was, on foreign territory, was forthwith without even an appearance of formal proceedings, handed back to the English ship. That is a gross breach of the international law, and a proof how far the subservience to England has brought proud France. The verdict of the court is as if no such breach of extra-territoriality had ever occurred.

The comments of the *Post* draw attention to the fact that the case of Savarkar had been settled not on the basis of any understandable legal framework but on the basis of pure politics—the dependence of France on the mercy of Britain. Though some papers in London felt a little peeved by the German onslaught, many others upheld what the *Post* had emphasized in no uncertain terms.

In his fiery editorial entitled "Savarkar Infamy," Guy A Aldred wrote in *The Herald of Revolt*:

Savarkar has been damned to a life of sojourn in an Indian dungeon by the infamy of a man who previously betrayed the French proletariat. But for the latter's agitation against the Hindu patriot's irregular arrest at Marseilles on July 8th last—and Briand's fears of a general strike—the French premier would never have invited the decision which brought about his resignation three days later. The Hague Award, annulling the Right of Asylum, was only possible because Aristid Briand voluntarily betrayed the sovereignty of France.

That the French premier was compelled to resign within days of the incident clearly indicates that the French people were angry with him for the manner in which the case had been handled and the outcome that it produced.

The editorial in the Belgium newspaper *La Society Nouvelle* wrote another fiery message: **"England's infamous empire rests on blood, ferocious repression and officially acknowledged systematic tyranny."**

The decision of the Hague trial came after the imprisonment awarded to Savarkar in India. The Colonial apparatus in India had put him out of action and the government of England made sure that the outcome at the Hague did not interfere with their planned destruction of Savarkar.

❑

Chapter 5

Gandhi Assassination Trial

Savarkar's detention and trial for being an accomplice in the conspiracy to murder Gandhi is an unfortunate accident, which happened only because of the malice that people holding high offices in the country had against him and his ideology. This has been revealed by scholars and writers who have investigated the circumstances in which the murder took place and confirmed later by the fact that after a year-long trial, the court acquitted him of all the charges that had been levelled against him. But prejudice against him is so deep-rooted that in spite of his honourable acquittal, some later-day writers, who have written about the murder, continue to propagate that he indeed was a part of the conspiracy and therefore guilty, and escaped punishment only because of the lackadaisical manner in which the Prosecution handled the case. It is, therefore, necessary to look at the circumstances in which the murder took place and how and why Savarkar was arrested, charged, tried, and eventually acquitted.

Nathuram Godse murdered Gandhi on January 30, immediately after he came out of his room to address his routine prayer meeting on the lawns of Birla House in Delhi. Godse, who was already in the midst of people who had gathered to hear him, moved close to him with his hands folded in a *namaskar*. Hidden within his hands was a pistol, which he brought out in a flash, and pumped three bullets into Gandhi, which caused his death within minutes.

This murder had actually been planned by Godse and his companion Narayan Apte for January 20. On that day, they and their other companions—Gopal Godse, Vishnu Karkare, Digambar Badge and Madanlala Pahwa—had come to Delhi with clearly defined roles for carrying out the murder.

The plan was that Pahwa would carry out an explosion to disrupt Gandhi's prayer meeting, which would lead to confusion among the people attending it. His companions would to take advantage of the confusion, explode grenades, and finish off Gandhi. But things did not work out the way they had planned.

Pahwa did carry out his part by exploding the bomb on that day, but the action that they had thought would follow the explosion did not happen. Pahwa's bomb exploded a little away from the prayer meeting. The people present there were prevented by Gandhi from running away from the place; in fact, he made them sit and stay calm. Confused by the turn of events, Pahwa's companions ran away from the scene just when he was overpowered and taken to the police station.

Realizing that it was not a good strategy to involve too many people to carry out the murder of Gandhi, Godse decided to do the job on his own.

Savarkar was not in the group that had come to Delhi on January 20, which clearly shows that he had no involvement in the murder. So the question: why was he implicated? Manohar Malgonkar, who wrote a book about the murder and the people involved in it in 1975, on the basis of extensive interviews with almost everybody who had anything to do with it—the culprits, the police, the officials and the lawyers—gives two hints about this in its revised edition, which came out in 2008.

Since the first edition of his book appeared during the times of Emergency imposed by Mrs Gandhi, when censorship on the spoken and written word was of the "utmost ruthlessness," Malgonkar writes that he was forced to "omit certain vital facts as, for instance," Dr Bhimrao Ambedkar's secret assurance to Mr L.B. Bhopatkar, that his client, Mr V. D. Savarkar had "been implicated as a murder-suspect on the flimsiest grounds" and that the confession that was instrumental in framing charges against the people involved in the crime was doctored by a magistrate, although his duty "was only to record what was said." The confession is a reference to the one made by Badge, who became an Approver in the case to secure pardon for himself.

These are just hints to which we will come again later. First, we will deal with the precise charges that were levelled against Savarkar, for which he was detained and hauled up in prison in Delhi for nearly a year, which ruined his health and brought a bad name to him. Though he had an honourable acquittal, some people, especially the politicians belonging to the leading political parties of the country, have continued to speak of him as a murderer. This makes it an example of what can only be called deep-rooted prejudice, which needs to be examined.

Much of the prejudice is actually related to the personality of Savarkar, his forthright views on the people involved in the freedom movement of the country and his avowed vision of the social and political culture of the country, which many politicians who came to power immediately after the independence of the country did not like.

But first about his involvement in the murder. In his long statement made before the court, Godse denied Savarkar's alleged involvement in Gandhi's murder: "I deny categorically what the Prosecution has so falsely maintained that I was guided in my action by Veer Savarkar and that, but for his complicity, I could never have acted in the way I have done. I take the strongest exception to this untrue and unjust charge and I further regard it as an insult to my intelligence and judgment. The Prosecution's attempt to make out that I was a mere tool in someone else's hands is an aspersion which is far from the truth. Indeed it is a perversion of it."

The Prosecution's case can be easily made out from this: that Savarkar secretly incited Godse and Apte to commit the murder but kept himself behind the scenes; so he was, in effect, the mastermind of the plot to kill Gandhi. The case rested on the fact of a long association between Godse and Savarkar and Badge's statement in which he stated that before leaving for Delhi on their mission to murder Gandhi, Godse and Apte went to see Savarkar at his home to seek his blessings, which he gave readily.

It is widely known and acknowledged by Godse himself that he had a long association with Savarkar. When the latter was transferred from the Celluar Jail in the Andamans to Ratnagiri, Godse was there at that time. Because of his revolutionary activities and his love for his motherland, Savarkar was well known and widely respected. Godse too loved him and admired him for the sacrifices he had made for the country. He also worked as his secretary for some time. When Savarkar was elected President of the Hindu Mahasabha, Godse felt supremely happy: "Millions of *Sanghatanists* looked up to him as the chosen hero, as the ablest and most faithful advocate of Hindu cause. I too was one of them. I worked devotedly to carry on the Mahasabha activities and hence came to be personally acquainted with Savarkarji."

When he and his friend Apte decided to start a newspaper, Savarkar helped by paying them fifteen thousand rupees, but he instructed them to convert the amount into shares, which they did. The office of the newspaper was also located in the lower floor of Savarkar's house. Because they had to run the newspaper, they had to go to his house every day, but this did not result in a regular contact. Godse says that Savarkar lived on the first floor, and "it was only very rarely that we could interview Veer Savarkar personally and that too by special appointment."

The Prosecution's case rested on this association between the two, and glossed over the differences that had grown between them right from that time to the time of India's independence, which find mention in Godse's statement, and were stated by Savarkar, too.

Godse's main complaint against Gandhi was about his thinking and activities *vis-à-vis* the Muslims of the country, and his persistent efforts, bordering on an unhealthy obsession, to please them, what he called the "sinister policy of communal favouritism," and his anti-Hindu stance, reflected in his condemnation of patriotic warriors like Shivaji, Rana Partap, and Guru Gobind Singh as "misguided patriots."

At first, Godse had believed that the Hindu Mahasabha would offer a fitting challenge to Gandhi's thinking and the activities that followed from this, but after some time he felt that he was wrong in this. He gives several examples to prove his point.

The first instance relates to Gandhi's reading of the *Quran* in a Hindu temple in the *Bhangi* colony of Delhi. Since he felt sure that Gandhi could not even dare to think of reading *Gita* in a mosque, Godse, along with Apte, arranged a demonstration against Gandhi's reading of the *Quran* in the temple of the colony. He had hoped that for this action he would be applauded by the *Sanghatan*, but, contrary to that, and also to his surprise, he earned a reprimand from Savarkar. He states that Savarkar called him and "blamed me privately for such anarchical tactics, even though this demonstration was peaceful. He said 'Just as I condemn the Congressites for breaking up your party meetings and election booths by disorderly conduct, I ought to condemn any such undemocratic conduct on the part of Hindu *Sanghatanist* also. If Gandhiji preached anti-Hindu teachings in his prayer meetings you should hold your party meetings and condemn his teachings. Amongst ourselves all different parties should conduct their propaganda on strictly constitutional lines.'"

Another incident relates to the stand that the party took on the issue of the Congress party forming a government in the country, which he did not like. "Veer Savarkar and other top-ranking Hindu Mahasabha leaders quickly and emphatically said that any Indian Government formed to conduct such a freed Indian state be no longer looked upon as the Government of a party—a Congress Government—but must be honoured and obeyed as a National Government of Hindustan and howsoever they deplored the creation of Pakistan their future motto should be a loyal and all-out support to the newly born Free Indian State. Thus, alone it would be possible to safeguard the newly won Freedom."

After this, Godse parted ways with Savarkar, for he says that "We felt in our heart of hearts that time had come when we should bid goodbye to Veer Savarkar's lead and cease to consult him in our future policy and programmes, nor should we confide to him our future plans."

Two other incidents renewed Godse's resolve to "act independently of the Mahasabha or its old veteran leaders. These are: (a) when Savarkar chose to fly the tricolour, the National Flag, along with the *Bhagwa* flag of the party on his house; and (b) when he expressed support to the National Government by congratulating them on their compromising attitude and asking Dr Mookerji to join the National Ministry.

In the light of these facts, the case of the Prosecution against Savarkar had no basis, for the warmth of Godse for Savarkar had cooled off. He had firmly resolved to deal with the threat that he felt Gandhi posed to the country on his own, without Savarkar's advice or blessing.

Because of this, the case of the Prosecution relied mainly on the statement given by Badge. Godse not only provided details to show how he had moved away from Savarkar and was not a mere tool in his hands, as the Prosecution had maintained, but also emphatically repudiated the testimony of Badge as well: "It is not true and it is totally false that either Mr Apte in my presence or I myself told Badge that Veer Savarkar had given us an order to finish Gandhiji, Nehru and Suhrawardy, as the approver is made to state falsely. It is not true that we ever took Badge to Veer Savarkar's house to take the last *Darshan* of Veer Savarkar in connection with any such plot or that Veer Savarkar ever said to us 'Be successful and come back, *'Yashasvi bhava.'* Neither Mr. Apte in my presence nor myself ever told Badge that Veer Savarkar told us that Gandhiji's ... years were over and therefore we were bound to be successful. I was neither so superstitious as to crave such blessings, nor so childish as to believe in such fore-telling."

This was endorsed by Karkare, too, when he said that "Badge is a liar, he is untrustworthy and has a habit of conjuring up stories."

For a better understanding of the falsity of the charges against Savarkar, which clearly indicate prejudice against him, it is essential to know what exactly happened after the murder of Gandhi by Godse.

Since Godse's links with the Hindu Mahasabha and RSS were quite well known, the offices of these two organizations were attacked and the shops and houses of the Hindu *Mahasabhites* were vandalized and burnt. Savarkar's house in Bombay was also attacked on January 31, but the furious mob was repelled by two of his aides till the police came on the scene. His bodyguard and personal secretary Apyakasar had been arrested hours before the raid on the house took place. His biographer Dhanajay Keer writes that "Savarkar also issued a statement on January 31, in which he said that the news of the assassination of Mahatma Gandhi was too shocking and sudden and he appealed to the people to stand by the Central Government of Free India and maintain order in the country."

On the same day, Savarkar's house was raided and all his private papers consisting of 143 files, containing around 10,000 letters, were seized by the police.

In the wake of investigations related to the murder, many people were arrested by the police from several locations. On February 5, 1948, Savarkar was put under house arrest. After that he was arrested and put in Arthur Road Jail in Bombay, even though just before that he had issued another statement condemning the act and also come out with a warning: "Let every patriotic citizen set to his heart the stern warning which history utters that a successful national revolution and a newly-born national State can have no worse enemy than a fratricidal civil war, especially so when it is encompassed from outside by alien hostility."

Savarkar remained in jail without being charged with any offence, but on March 11, he was arrested again by the Delhi police under a warrant from the Delhi Presidency Magistrate on the charge of being one of the conspirators in the murder of Gandhi, and was produced before the Chief Presidency Magistrate of Bombay for a further remand.

S. V. Deodhar, a local advocate, and a staunch supporter of Savarkar, made an application for his bail, which was rejected. Since the property of Savarkar that had been confiscated during the British times had not been returned to him even after the country became free and had its own government, questions regarding this were also raised in the Bombay Legislative Council, but with no result.

On May 15, 1948, Savarkar was named one of the accused in the murder of Gandhi. All the accused, who were in Bombay till then, were brought to Delhi on May 24 and imprisoned in the Red Fort. A part of the Fort was converted into a Court, where the trial opened on May 27. Sadly, this happened to be the eve of his 65th birthday and he suffered from multiple health disorders.

Savarkar was charged under several sections: 120/BIPC, 115 and 302 IPC and Section 109 IPC. He was defended by a large group of lawyers, headed by Bhopatkar.

The recording of the prosecution evidence began on June 24 and continued till November 6. One forty-nine witnesses were produced by the prosecution; 404 documentary exhibits and 80 material exhibits were also produced in the court. The hearing of the arguments began on December 1 and continued till December 30. P R Patna argued the case on behalf of Savarkar.

The judgment was delivered on February 10, 1949. All the accused, except Savarkar, were found guilty on one count or the other. They were told that they could appeal against their conviction and sentence within fifteen days.

We have already seen how Godse in his statement traced his gradual moving away from Savarkar's position and how he emphatically said that Badge had lied all the time about his involvement in the crime. But it seemed that this was not enough to free Savarkar from the charges levelled against him.

Savarkar had to make a long statement in his defense, and it is important that people know about that, especially because later writers like Tushar Gandhi proclaimed him guilty in spite of all evidence to the contrary.

We present here some key parts of his defense to show how the element of prejudice has grown over time because of his person and not because of his direct or indirect involvement in the murder, which makes attack on him a case of *ad hominem* attack.

Savarkar began his defense by denying the charges levelled against him. He talked about his career, traced his association with the Hindu Mahasabha and the circumstances in which he came into contact with Godse, and stated that he supported the newspaper started by Godse and Apte because it was a Mahasabha party paper. He provided financial and moral help not just to their paper *Agrani*, but to many other papers too; these included *Vikram* and *Free Hindusthan*. At no stage and in no circumstances did he ever accept "the responsibility to identify myself with the policy and the control of the *Agrani*."

The basis of Savarkar's association with Godse and Apte was their Mahasabha connection and they were "neither specially chosen not exclusively trusted" by him. They, in fact, wanted to develop this exclusivity by wanting him to write special articles for their newspaper, but he did not. The reason was that the editors of many other papers too wanted him to write for them, and because he could not write for all, he did not write for *Agrani*, too: "I would have been held partial if I wrote to some and failed to write for others." All this is clearly reflected in his correspondence with Godse and Apte.

After clarifying the nature of his contact with Godse and Apte, Savarkar offered a point-by-point rebuttal of what Badge had put in his statement about his complicity in the crime. Being a lawyer by training, he responded to the charges not only by plain denial but also by proving them wrong by using his argumentative skills.

Firstly, about Badge's allegation that Savarkar met Godse and Apte on January 17. He stated that he did not meet them on that day nor on any other day, and so he had no occasion to speak the words attributed to him, including the oft quoted sentence "Be successful and come back."

Secondly, even if what Badge says about the visit can be believed to be true, that cannot be held against him. The fact is that Badge could not have known what transpired in his meeting with Godse and Apte, because he himself said that he was not with them in Savarkar's room that was on the first floor, and all the time he stayed on the ground floor.

Thirdly, even if Badge's assertion that when the two came downstairs from Savarkar's room along with him and spoke the words attributed to him are believed to be true, that does not prove anything. These words could have been spoken in the context of any other situation, issue, or problem and not necessarily in the context of the impending murder. Since Badge was away from the scene, he could not know the exact context in which these words were spoken.

Fourthly, Badge's saying that Apte told him about the sentence spoken by Savarkar while they were driving cannot be held against him. Badge had not heard the words directly spoken by him, but from Apte. It could be that Apte was lying or just bragging. Therefore, it can only be called hearsay and not evidence against him.

Fifthly, both Godse and Apte positively deny that they ever spoke these sentences to Badge. In fact, they deny that the incident involving their meeting with Savarkar ever took place.

Sixthly, Badge had also mentioned in his statement that they had visited Savarkar's home in a taxi, but the taxi driver, who had been brought to corroborate his story, could not give any details about Savarkar's house. Besides, there was a marked variation in the timing of events in their statements, which makes the taxi driver's evidence unreliable.

So Savarkar concluded that Badge's statement "consists mostly of fabrications," and his "motive in giving false evidence against me is clear. He saw that the police were working frantically on the basis of some shadowy suspicions, they had to rope me in this case by hook or by crook." Since the police was looking for some "sensational publicity and self-advertisement for themselves," Badge thought that by getting Savarkar implicated in the murder, he could also save his skin.

Savarkar also picked several parts of Badge's statement to prove that he was unscrupulous and capable of speaking falsehoods to save himself. These are: he sold bombs and other explosive materials without a proper license; he hid revolvers in a taxi without the knowledge of its driver, because in case something went wrong, the blame could be put on the driver and not on him; he travelled without tickets and bribed ticket collectors; and he made false representations to obtain money.

In a similar vein, Savarkar tore into the evidence provided by other witnesses. For example, the Prosecution produced three letters, two written by Madanlal to him and the third containing a receipt sent by Badge to his secretary. Savarkar argued that these had no connection, whatsoever, with the murder.

Similarly, there were two or three sentences in the testimony of Miss Modak in which she said that she overheard Apte and Godse talking about their intended visit to his place on January 14. This evidence too did not prove anything because she herself said that she "did not see them actually entering the Savarkar Sadan."

Savarkar also refuted point-by-point the story alleged to have been told by Madanlal to Dr Jain that he had gone to see Savarkar and that he had commended him for his exploits in Ahmednagar, patted his back and told him to "carry on." He argued that this meeting had never taken place. After telling Jain about his exploits in Ahmednagar he had also told him that his party was plotting against the life of some leader. By narrating his exploits in Ahmednagar in conjunction with the plot to murder some leader, he had tried to give the impression as if the idea of the plot also came from him. But Jain in his statement admitted that "he did not know from Madanalal the names of his party members, nor other details and knew himself next to nothing about it." Besides, the story given by Jain was just based on his memory, which invariably is unreliable. So Savarkar concluded that Jain's account has no "evidentiary value against me as it fails to connect me individually in any way whatsoever with this alleged conspiracy."

Savarkar also referred to the evidence given by Angad Singh and Mr Desai, Home Minister, and argued that what they had said was based on hearsay and therefore not admissible as evidence under Section 157 I.E.A.

Savarkar also exposed the falsity of the Prosecution's claim that they had overwhelming documentary evidence against him. He stated that this evidence consisted of 143 files that contained more than 10,000 letters, which were removed from his home at the time of his arrest and put in the CID office in Bombay. The police Inspector A R Pradhan admitted that he worked on these files for full three months and went through all of them, but could not find anything incriminating against him. He had isolated only 100 to 125 letters, which related to the correspondence between him and Godse and Apte. Out of these, twenty letters written by Godse and Apte to him were admitted as prosecution exhibits, only to establish their connection with him.

Savarkar himself quoted copiously from these letters to show that the two were associated with him only because of their connection with the *Hindu Sanghatan* and its activities, which were "perfectly public, legitimate and legal." Therefore, the letters did not prove anything against him. He quoted from Sarkar's Evidence Act, Section 10, page 98, which lays down that "The evidence of an accused's association with any of the conspirators would not be enough by itself to convict him of being one of the parties to that conspiracy."

Savarkar concluded that the Prosecution's attempt to make much of his association with Godse and Apte and to "assert dogmatically that Godse and Apte must have consulted me beforehand regarding this conspiracy and that but for my sanction the crime would not have been committed at all... [is] absurd." Their respect and loyalty towards him was like that of thousands of other workers towards him.

Apart from exposing the falsity of the Prosecution's case against him on purely legal grounds, which he calls "the negative side of my defence," Savarkar also dwelt on the nature of his relationship with Gandhi, which he calls "the positive side of my defence." This part of the defence has some salutary lessons for the political class of our country, which are relevant to our times as well.

Savarkar dwelt at length on how he met Gandhi in London, and how they were "friends," and how later Gandhi wrote kind notes about him in *Young India*. The burden of these disclosures was to emphasize that "in spite of fundamental differences in our ideologies on some points and in virtue of close affinity on others, there ever continued a mutual respect for and a personal goodwill to each other."

Savarkar also quoted extensively from his press statements issued from time to time in which he praised the efforts of leaders like Nehru and Gandhi and also raised concern over the fasts of Gandhi that he undertook "even at the risk of his life," and said that "his precious life at this juncture is of immeasurably greater value than his loss to it."

This part of the defence also makes it quite clear that though he was a revolutionary who advocated violence as a legitimate weapon to fight for one's freedom from external control, violence had no place in a free democratic polity. We have already seen a brief glimpse of this in the reprimand that he gave to Godse and Apte when they tried to disrupt Gandhi's meeting. Here he says that the, "revolutionary mentality which was inevitable and justifiable while we were struggling against an alien and armed oppression, must be instantly changed into a constitutional one if we wanted to save our State from dangerous party strife and civil wars."

This part also clarifies that Savarkar loved his country above everything else. He wanted that it should grow strong, and it did not matter who governed it. This speaks a great deal about the political culture that he wanted to see grow in our country, something that has deteriorated over the years, because politicians crave only for power and often lose sight of the country. In public discourse, they have become abusive and do not hesitate to attack each other.

Savarkar also mentioned how he exhorted all the Hindu leaders in 1947 to "get united and since India had attained its independence, all parties should sink their differences and strengthen and support the Indian State."

Because of this, younger people in the Hindu Mahasabha did not like what they called the "old lead" of the organization. That is why Godse and Apte used their newspaper to make continuous attacks "on the failure of the Mahasabha under its old leaders to defend Hindudom and kept exhorting Hindu youths to form an independent 'Council of Action' wherein the 'old lead' should have no hand whatsoever."

The statements of Godse and Savarkar and his elaborate defence clearly proves that Savarkar was not involved in the conspiracy at all. So the all-important question: why was he arrested, charged, and imprisoned?

We have already hinted at the two reasons that contributed to Savarkar's arrest, but the question that we need to answer is: why did the police need to do that?

The fact is that the police had acted incompetently and wanted to make up for that lack. Between the time when Madanlal Pahwa was arrested in Delhi on 20 January and the time of the murder of Gandhi on 30 January, the police in Delhi and Bombay did not act in unison; their effort lacked clarity of purpose and they hardly showed any sense of urgency. In fact, if we look closely at the working of the police from the two locations, we find that there was no unified plan to act promptly, although Pahwa had told the Delhi police that the people who were with him would return.

The police chief of Bombay Nagarvala had a fanciful idea that there was a big conspiracy not to kill but to "'kidnap Mahatma Gandhi. It was a very big organization, with about twenty principal conspirators, each assisted by twenty persons and in possession of considerable quantities of firearms and other lethal weapons.'"

So when the murder took place, the police started clutching at every little thing that could implicate some big name. The desperation that characterized their effort can be seen from what happened on the 20th of January. During their first attempt to murder Gandhi on the 20th, Godse and Apte went to the Hindu Mahasabha office in New Delhi to check on the arrival of their accomplices on 19th January. They also met its Secretary, Ashutosh Lahiri, from whose office a trunk call was booked at 9.20 a.m. and the number called was that of Savarkar's house. Nobody knows who booked the call and for what purpose. But the police investigators held that it was made by Godse to find out if Gopal Godse had passed through Bombay.

Malgonkar's comment on this is: "This was all of a piece with their general belief that all the conspirators received instructions or at least blessings from Savarkar before they proceeded to Delhi. Gopal maintained stoutly to the author that he did not even know where Savarkar's house was." The police stuck to their theory although the call did not come through and was cancelled after about two hours.

Since the police wanted to prove what they believed to be true, they needed a statement from somebody among the conspirators to support their contention. So they roped in the weak link of the team: Badge. We have already seen how his testimony was refuted by both Godse and Savarkar because it was totally based on lies. The over-eagerness of the police to make him say exactly what they wanted was so overdone that it looked totally incredible. That is why Malgonkar remarks that "Badge's amazing ability to remember every single thing that happened within his sight or hearing during those days is itself suspicious; his performance as a witness was so flawless as to resemble that of an actor who has studied his lines thoroughly and never fumbles for a word.... An interesting sidelight on Badge's brilliant performance as a witness is provided by Shankar in his testimony. Even in custody, Shankar was subjected to almost incessant coaching by Badge as to what precisely he was required to say in court. He has some pertinent revelations to make about how industriously Badge himself was practising his lines."

We have an interesting report on the political dimension of Savarkar's alleged involvement in the murder of Gandhi which was made by his lawyer Bhopatkar in a volume published by the Savarkar Memorial Committee on February 16, 1989. He reveals how during his stay in the Hindu Mahasabha office, he got a call from Ambedkar to meet him on the sixth milestone on the Mathura Road. He met him at the appointed place, and moved into his car, which he was driving himself. At one point, he "stopped the car and told Bhopatkar: 'There is no real charge against your client; quite worthless evidence has been concocted. Several members of the cabinet were strongly against it, but to no avail. Even Sardar Patel could not go against these orders. But take it from me, there just is no case. You will win.'" "Who...Jawaharlal Nehru?... But why?" A clear case of political vendetta.

Now the prejudice. Prejudice is either blind or works through false logic. We have instances of both in the case of Savarkar. The first one is associated with Nagarvala. Even when Savarkar was acquitted because there was no case against him, Nagarvala continued to believe in his pet theory, which he told Malgonkar: "'To my dying day I shall believe that Savarkar was the man who organized Gandhi's murder.'" What could be more unreasonable than that?

The second is associated with Tushar Gandhi who uses a fallacious mode of reasoning to prove that Savarkar was really the mastermind of the plot. He builds a negative portrait of Savarkar to pronounce him guilty.

The first point he states in the Foreword to his book is that Gandhi's murder was the culmination of a series of earlier attempts on Gandhi's life: "Does anyone know that there were four recorded attempts on Gandhi's life before the last two on the 20th and 30th of January 1948? Four of the five failed attempts were made at a time when Pakistan was not even on the agenda of the Muslim League. All the four attacks were made by the extreme Right-wing upper caste Hindus of Poona; three of the four attempts on his life were made by the Narayan Apte-Godse Gang and Nathuram was caught in two of those attempts."

He also says that the Congress government and "at least some of the members of the Cabinet were fed up of the interventions of the meddlesome old man. To them, a martyred Mahatma would be easier to live with. **According to a secret report submitted to the Home Minister Sardar Patel, many in the police force and many bureaucrats were secret members of the RSS and the Hindu Mahasabha, and were actively supporting and promoting the ideology of the Hindu extremist organisations."**

And then he comments on the trial. "The prosecution was lackadaisical; it felt that the trial was prejudged. Savarkar had to be exonerated at any cost, the rest were pre-condemned."

The conclusion is clear. Hindu extremism was a strong force which had its influence in the government, and because its leader was Savarkar, he had to be saved anyhow. So the trial was a mere eyewash.

If Tarun Gandhi had his way, he would not allow the guilty ones even to speak, for he thinks that their statements were only expressions of anger: "The most surprising aspect was that Godse was allowed to give vent to his anger in court twice; once at the Red Fort and again during the appeal in the Punjab High Court." He also says that it is "definitely not written by Godse," and "smacks of the penmanship of Savarkar." Keeping in view the contents of the two statements, this assertion is totally absurd.

While developing the connection between Godse and Savarkar, Tushar Gandhi writes that "Savarkar had begged for clemency from the King Emperor after spending fourteen years in the Cellular Jail.... In return of a promise of obedience and loyalty to the British and good conduct, Savarkar was shifted to Ratnagiri..." (16). Keer has more than six pages in Sarvarkar's biography on the efforts that individuals and organizations made to seek his transfer to India.

When Savarkar told his party workers to work for the British during the war, Tushar Gandhi comments that "Savarkar felt this was his opportunity to get close to the British." (19). Savarkar was always against the British and he went to jail for this. He wanted people to join the war because they could get military training, which would be useful to the country in future. He had no personal axe to grind. Savarkar's stand on this was approved even by Subhash Bose, which we have already quoted in Chapter 1.

At another place Tushar remarks that Savarkar was, "the first Indian leader to publicly say that India could never be a united country." But the facts are to the contrary. Savarkar and Hindu Mahasabha were against the partition of the country and always thought of India as *Akhand Bharat*. Besides, one of the arguments given by Godse in his defence was that by murdering Gandhi, **he only fulfilled his wish. He had himself proclaimed that India's partition would be over his dead body. Since the partition had taken place when he was still alive, so he completed the unfinished task.**

Tushar Gandhi also gives credence to the doctored confession of Badge to strengthen his view that Savarkar was a bad man whose views were opposed to that of Gandhi and he all the time urged people to get rid of him. The earlier attempts on Gandhi's life and the last one too was the result of his instigating the rabid Hindu youth of Maharashtra. We have already seen how untrue Badge's statement is.

Tushar's prejudice is so deep-rooted that he sees even ordinary happenings as pointers to justify his assertions. When the trial opened at Red Fort on May 27, Bhopatkar told the court that because Savarkar was frail and not in good health, he be provided a "comfortable, cushioned chair." Tushar considers this a part of the strategy of his lawyer to "separate him from the other accused and use every ploy to strengthen his argument that Savarkar was not involved in the murder or conspiracy in any manner." What could be flimsier than that!

Savarkar's arrest and trial will be remembered as a blot on the government of the day that got him embroiled in it to tarnish his image and destroy whatever he did for his country. It was a sinister plot concocted only to malign him. The most regrettable aspect of this is that the country for which he willingly gave his lifeblood and suffered as no other leader did, treated him worse than his enemies.

At several places in the narrative of these trials we have indicated how Savarkar's views are different from what quite often are held about him by a host of political persons, educated as well as uneducated, in our times, a continuation of the campaign to belittle his contribution in the making of the country. In fact, his main difference with Gandhi was that his policies were divisive in nature, even though he might not have thought them to be, for they eventually led to the partition of the country. Savarkar wanted India to remain a single united entity and become a strong and vibrant country. Addressing the Hindu Mahasabha Session in 1937, Savarkar said: "Let the Indian state be purely Indian. Let it not recognise any invidious distinction whatsoever as regards the franchise, public services, offices, taxation on the grounds of religion and race. Let no cognisance be taken whatsoever of a man being Hindu or Mohammedan, Christian, or Jew. Let all citizens of that Indian state be treated according to their worth irrespective of their religion or racial percentage in the general population."

The government that was in power in 1948 totally disregarded this laudable thought by creating small and big islands of privilege and special treatment. And these, as we have seen, have grown over the years, because it suited the Congress party to stay in power. We have already seen how this has led to social disharmony among the people of our country. The irony is that many leaders continue to associate Savarkar with divisive thinking which they themselves employ unabashedly in the name of this and that ism.

❑

Appendixes

Two Flags of Savarkar

We are not sure how well this fact is known that the first flag of 'Free India' and the first ever to be hoisted outside India was Savarkar's concept and creation. It was specially designed for the International Socialist Congress held at Stuttgart in Germany on August 22, 1907.

In London, Savarkar's major concern was to organize campaigns to project the colonial oppression of his people and mobilize world opinion in his favour. But when one day news reached India House that a meeting of the International Socialist Congress was to be held at Stuttgart in Germany on 22 August, 1907, Savarkar seized on this opportunity of getting a foreign forum to arouse the conscience of the western world. Madam Cama and Sardar Singh Rana were chosen to represent India at the Conference. They were listed among the 123 delegates from Great Britain and they were sponsored by H M Hyndman of the Socialist Democratic Federation who himself presented his celebrated report entitled "The Ruin of India by British Rule."

Despite stiff opposition from and eventual walkout by Ramsay Mcdonald, the British representative, who later became the Prime Minister of England, Madam Cama, supported by Maurice Hyndman of England, Boekel of Germany, and Jean Jaures of France, moved a resolution on Indian freedom and unfurled the Flag of Free India at the Conference.

Holding the flag in her hand, Madam Cama marched to the dais of the august house and thundered:

> This flag is of Indian Independence. Behold, it is born. It is already sanctified by the blood of martyred Indian youth: I call upon you, gentlemen, to rise and salute the flag of Indian Independence. In the name of this flag I appeal to lovers of freedom all over the world to cooperate with this flag in freeing one-fifth of the human race.

Up stood the delegates and saluted the flag of Indian Independence.

The flag prepared by Madam Cama from her silk sari is safely preserved with Shri Rajendra Singh Rana, the grandson of S.S. Rana and five time M.P. from Bhavnagar (Gujarat). It consists of three horizontal stripes of equal width, similar in colour to the red, white and blue of the French flag. According to Emily Brown, "the three colours were green (the sacred colour of the Muslims), the centre band saffron or golden (the sacred colour of the Buddhists and Sikhs), and the lower string being the Hindu red. 'Vande Matram' was embroidered in Sanskrit on the centre gold band." The top section had eight stars in a row, the middle section had sun on the left and the moon on the right. Highly symbolic, the stars represented the eight provinces of India while the sun and the moon stood for the Hindus and Muslims respectively. Thus, the flag was truly national and secular.

The Hindu Dhawaja

In contrast to this is the other flag of Savarkar, popularly known as the *Hindu dhawaja,* which shows his exalted and epic concept of a flag and its philosophy. It was hoisted at the 1929 session of the Hindu Mahasabha at Surat and later accepted for good (with the addition of *Swastik*). It is triangular in *bhagwa* (saffron) bearing *Kundalini, Kripan,* Omkar and Lotus. While Kundalini (with Om and Lotus) is the symbol of *Nihshreyas* (spiritual bliss), the *Kripan* is the symbol of *Abhyudaya* (worldly prosperity). Elaborating this in a pamphlet entitled *Hindu Dhawaja*, Savarkar said:

The Kundalini represents all the ultimate aspirations, feelings and powers of mankind and the *Kripan* represents the all-sided *Abhyudaya* aiming at and leading to the nation's ideal prosperity. These two alone, being depicted on the national flag, will be able to indicate and inspire the ideals of *Abhyudaya* and *Nihshreyas*.

The one represents the highest bliss, the other worldly prosperity; they combine *Shanti* and *Shakti, Yoga* and *Bhoga, Nivritti* and *Pravaritti, Dhyeya* and *Dharana*; the one symbolizes *Aupanishadic Vidya* (highest spiritual attainment, the other denotes *Aupanishadic Avidya* worldly advancement; the former reminds one of *Yogeshwar Krishna,* the latter of *Dhanurdhara Partha* of the *Geeta*; the *Kundalini* means *DhyanYoga* and the *Kripan* means *Karma Yoga*.

In order that kingdom, power and glory may not become polluted by the actions of tyranny and to keep the central truth of virtuous conduct always before mankind, the background of the Hindu flag is made of *bhagwa*—the red ochre colour. This is the colour of renunciation. There is no *Tyaga* without *Yoga* and *Kshema*. Therefore, the *Kripan* is for the *Yoga Kshema*. In the same way the *Omkar* is the sacred name of the Great one with whom the liberated souls become one in the highest state of *Nihshreyas* of *Vedic*, non-*Vedic Sanatani* and modern Hindus.

Be there everlasting victory and eternal life to the Hindu flag bearing the symbol of *Kundalini* with *Omkar* and *Kripan* from this end to that end of the world flying with the prowess of millions of warriors accomplishing the highest happiness of all mankind.

❑

Two Tracts of Savarkar

Of the several tracts that Savarkar wrote and circulated in England, the most profound ones are "O Martyrs" (1908) and "Choose, Oh Indian Princes" (1909). The second has been dug out by Shridhar Damle from a library in Chicago. The two pieces are typical of Savarkar's epic style, classic idiom and the perfect choice of titles and sub-titles. They also provide evidence of Savarkar the seer and visionary: the first one of India's imminent independence and the second one of his strong faith in parliamentary democracy.

O' Martyrs

The battle of freedom once begun
And handed down from sire to son
Though often lost is ever won!!

Today is the 10th of May! It was on this day that, in the ever memorable year of 1857, the first campaign of the war of independence was opened by you, O'Martyrs, on the battlefields of India. The Motherland, awakened to the sense of her degrading slavery, unsheathed her sword, burst forth the shackles and struck the first blow for her liberty and for her honour. It was on this day that the war cry *"Maro Firungee Ko"* was raised by the throats of thousands. It was on this day that the Sepoys of Meerut, having risen in a terrible uprising, marched down to Delhi, saw the waters of Jamuna glittering in the sunshine, caught one of those historical moments which close the past epoch to introduce a new one, and "had found, in a moment, a leader, a flag, and cause, and converted the mutiny into a national and religious war."

All honour be to you O' Martrys, for it was for the preservation of the honour of the race that you performed the fiery ordeal of a revolution when the religions of the land were threatened with a forcible and sinister conversion, when the hypocrite threw off his friendly garb and stood up in the naked heinousness of a perfidious foe breaking treaties, smashing crowns, forging chains and mocking all the while our merciful mother for the very honesty with which she believed the pretensions of the white liar. Then you, O' Martyrs of 1857, awoke the mother, inspired the mother, and for the mother, rushed to the battlefield terrible and tremendous with the war cry *"Maro Firugee Ko"* on your lips, and with sacred *mantra*, God and *Hindustan* on your banner. Well did you do in rising. For otherwise, although your blood might have been spared, yet the stigma of servility would have been the deeper, one more link would have been added to the cursed chain of demoralizing patience, and the world would have again contemptuously pointed to our nation saying, "She deserves slavery, she is happy in slavery. For, even in 1857 she did not raise even a finger to protect her interest and her honour."

This day, therefore, we dedicate, O'Maryrs, to your inspiring memory. It was on this day that you raised a new flag to be upheld, you uttered a mission to be fulfilled, you saw a vision to be realized, you proclaimed a nation to be born.

We take up your cry, we revere your flag, we are determined to continue that fiery mission of "away with the foreigner," which you uttered amidst the prophetic thunderings of the revolutionary war. Revolutionary, yes, it was a revolutionary war, for the war of 1857 shall not cease till the revolution arrives, striking slavery into dust, elevating liberty to the throne. Whenever a people rises for its freedom, whenever that seed of liberty gets germinated in the blood of its father, and whenever there remains at least one true son to avenge that blood of his father, there never can be an end to such a war as this. No, a revolutionary war knows no truce, save liberty or death. We, inspired by your memory, determine to continue the struggle you began in 1857; we refuse to acknowledge the armistice as a truce; we look upon the battles you fought as the battles of the first campaign—the defeat of which cannot be the feat of the war. What? Shall the world say that India has accepted the defeat as the final one? That the blood of 1857 was shed in vain? That the Sons of India betray their fathers' vows? No, by *Hindustan*, No! The historical continuity of the Indian nation is not cut off. The war begun on the 10th of May 1857 is not over on the 10th of May 1908, nor shall it ever cease till a 10th of May to come sees the destiny accomplished, sees the beautiful India crowned, either with the lustre of victory or with the halo of Martyrdom.

But, O' glorious Martyrs, in this pious struggle of yours, help us by your inspiring presence. Torn in innumerable petty selves, we cannot realize the grand unity of the Mother. Whisper, then, unto us by what magic you caught the secret of Union. How the *Firungee* rule was shattered to pieces and the Swadeshi thrones were set up by the common consent of Hindus and Mahomedans. How the higher love of the Mother united the difference of castes and creeds, how the venerated and the venerable Bahadur Shah prohibited the killing of cows throughout India, how Shrimant Nana Sahib, after the first salute of thundering cannon to the Emperor of Delhi, reserved for himself the second one. How you staggered the whole world by uniting under the banner of the Mother and forced your enemies to say. "Among the many lessons the Indian mutiny conveys to the historian and administrator, none is of the greater importance than the warning that it is possible to have a Revolution in which Brahmins and Shudras, Mahomedans and Hindus were united against us and that it is not safe to suppose that the peace and stability of our domination in any great measure depends on the continent being inhabited by different races with different religious systems, for they mutually understand each other and respect and take part in each other's modes and ways of doings. The Mutiny reminds us that our domination rests on a thin crust ever likely to be rent by titanic fires of social changes and revolutions."

Whisper unto us the nobility of such an alliance of Religion and Patriotism, the true religion which is on the side of patriotism, the true patriotism which secures the freedom of religion. And give us the marvellous energy, daring and secrecy with which you organized the mighty volcano; show us the volcanic magma that underlies the green thin crust, on which the foe is to be kept lulled into a false security; tell how the *'chapati'*—that fiery cross of India—flew from village to village and from valley to valley setting the whole intellect of the nation on fire by the very vagueness of its message and then let us hear the roaring thunder with which the volcano at last burst forth, with an all-shattering force, rushing, smashing, burning and consuming into one continuous fiery flow of red-hot lava-flood; city after city, regiment after regiment, prince after prince, sepoys, police, *zamindars, pandits, maulvis,* the multiple headed Revolution sounded its tocsin and temples and mosques resounded with the cry, *"Maro Firungee Ko...."* (away with the foreigners). Meerut rose, Delhi rose, Benares, Agra, Patna, Lucknow, Allahabad, Jagdalpore, Jhansi, Banda, Indore—from Peshawar to Calcutta and from Narmada to the Himalayas, the volcano burst forth into a sudden, simultaneous and all-consuming conflagration.

And then, O'Martyrs, tell us the little as well as the great defects which you found out in our people in the great experiment of yours. But, above all, point out that most ruinous, nay, the only material drawback in the body of the nation which rendered all your efforts futile—the mean selfish blindness which refuses to see its way to join the Nation's cause. Say that the only cause of the defeat of Hindustan was Hindustan herself, that shaking away the slumber of centuries, the Mother rose to hit the foe, but while her right hand was striking the "*Firungees* dead," her left hand struck, alas, not the enemy but her own forehead! So she staggered and fell back into the inevitable swoon of fifty years.

Fifty years are past, but, O' restless hearts, behold that your Golden Jubilee shall not pass without seeing your wishes fulfilled! We have heard your voice and we gather courage from it. With limited means you sustained a war, not against tyranny alone but against the tyranny and treachery together. The *Doab* and *Ayodhya*, making a united stand, waged a war not only against the whole of British power but against the rest of India too: and you fought for three years and yet had well-nigh snatched away the crown of Hindustan and smashed the hollow existence of the alien rule. What an encouragement this! What the *Doab* and *Ayodhya* could do in a month, the simultaneous, sudden and determined rising of the whole of Hindustan can do in a day. This hope illumines our hearts and assures us of success. And so we avow that your Golden Jubilee year shall not pass without seeing the resurging India making a triumphant entry into the world.

For, the bones of a Bahadur Shah are crying vengeance from their grave. The spirit of Mangal Pandey is still beckoning from the scaffold for the fulfilment of the sacred mission. For the blood of the dauntless Luxmi Bai is boiling with indignation. The solemn affirmation of Kunwar Singh to shatter to pieces the British rule is still echoing in the air of Hindustan. The streaks of blood that flowed from Azim Ullah and Pir Ali Shah have left an indelible impression on the pages of history. For Veer Tatia Tope, when he was going to the gallows for having refused to admit his crime and to divulge the secrets of the conspiracy, whispered defiance to the *"Firungee,"* and said in prophetic words:

'You may hang me today, you may hang such as me every day, but thousands will still rise in my place—your object will never be gained.'

Indians, these words must be fulfilled. Your blood, O'Martyrs shall be avenged.

Vande Matram

❑

Choose, Oh Indian Princes!

Is She Not Your Mother Too...?

The general upheaval of the National Spirit that is now stirring in the hearts of the Indian people to find an adequate expression has produced a sense of insecurity and fear in the minds of the princes of India. The prosecutions and persecutions ordered against this Revolutionary spirit by the Rajas and Maharajas of India have not dismayed us, the members of *Abhinava Bharat*, as their actions have in no way created any new set of circumstances that are likely to hamper its progress to any appreciable extent. On the contrary, the very fact that these exalted chiefs should be forced to leave their self-centred dignity and indifference, and betray signs of fear and consternation is a distinct gain to the cause, inasmuch as it is a recognition, though forced, by the most haughty and listless Aristocracy of the world, that this New Birth has already outgrown the stage of negligible insignificance and has assumed a power and a following which can no longer be conveniently brushed aside. The Maharajas of Kashmir, of Kolhapur, of Jaipur and a host of minor principalities have heaped anathemas upon this Infant Revolution, whilst the Maharaja of Gwalior has inflicted most atrocious punishments on more than twenty young patriots for having taken up the flag of *Abhinava Bharat*. Want of mutual understanding and the instinct of self-preservation seem to have evoked this antipathy of the Indian princes towards the *Abhinava Bharat*, and, therefore, in order to remove that antipathy and reassure those princes, it is necessary that the line of action that is likely to be adopted by the Young Indians towards the princely element in the land should once for all be clearly and definitely pronounced.

Abhinava Bharat

They mistake greatly who look upon this *Abhinava Bharat* as a secret society or a party of violence, manufactured in the western patterns. The *Abhinava Bharat* is not a movement of mushroom growth. It was not planned by the young men of Gwalior, nor can it be crushed by the Maharaja of Gwalior. *Abhinava Bharat* is a principle, a truth, as deeply embedded in the sinews of the Motherland as are her mountains or her rivers. It was this very principle that inspired Shri Rama and Shri Krishna, that inspired Chandragupta when he drove the Grecians, that inspired Vikrama when he routed the *Sakas*. It is reborn from time to time. But it is reborn not in the sense of being born again but only in the sense of reasserting itself. A secret society or a party your ... laws might crush, but a Truth exists in order not to be crushed but to crush.

Abhinava Bharat has a reverence for our great past as profound as it has an ambition for a greater future. It believes that the future of India must not be an outlandish grafting of a dead tree, but in India's own past is the *Dharmas* of India's being and that it cannot and will not break-up the continuity of its nationalist life any more than it can break the continuity of the stream of the Ganges. And thus our programmes of the future will be a natural evolution growing out of the past, assimilating and consolidating the new and healthy elements of the time, without any sudden or abrupt innovation or apish and ruinous imitations.

Our Ideal of State

The princes of India need not be anxious about the

mysterious policy and the republican tendency of the revolutionary element in India's young heart. For, our ideal of state does not imply any fanatical and blind attachment to the theoretical excellence of a particular political organisation. No one but the voice of the Mother Herself will and can determine, when once she comes to Herself and stands free, what constitution should be adopted by Her for the guidance of Her life, after the revolution is over. Without usurping this, Her sacred authority, we want just to point out what it is that the *Abhinava Bharat* for itself wants to aim at. We believe that history has proved to demonstration that the different forms of constitution, like any other instruments, depend for their effectiveness each upon the prevalence of a particular set of circumstances. A sword, though most effective in the battlefield, can neither saw wood nor pare nails. Republic of monarchy, democracy or aristocracy are forms which, when blindly followed irrespective of time or place, lead to destruction. Without going into details about the suitability of this or that form of state for India, a subject which, important though it is, can only be dealt with separately and not here, we might mention this much that whether the head of the imperial Government of the Indian Nation be a President or a King depends upon how the Revolution develops itself. We are not particular, we are not fanatically attached to either of these forms. They are mere names and we do not quarrel about them. But to one thing alone we are fanatically attached. One thing alone we will neither exchange nor compromise. We will risk our lives, we will devote our energy, we will not lay down our sword, till we see that that thing is triumphant over all. We will fight as doggedly for the constructive success of that principle as for the destruction of the foreign tyrant. For we know that the mission of the Revolution will not be complete and its necessity will not be removed unless and until this mighty principle stands supreme in the land, obeyed by all, worshipped by all, and carried into execution—it matters not whether by a President or a Monarch. And that principle is that the Mother's voice is the voice of the majority of the Indian people, freely asked and freely ascertained. All laws must be determined and sanctioned by the voice of the people. For the highest aim of all Government being the greatest good of the greatest number—good, not only in the material sense of profit and loss, but also in the highest ethical and spiritual sense of the word—the parliamentary Government is the only effective and essential condition to realise the ultimate ideal of a state. We shall therefore uncompromisingly insist upon the attainment of the Parliamentary constitution under which the people's voice shall be the Dictator of all laws in the land, thinking it immaterial, and even to some extent harmful to be rigid and fanatic as to the other formal questions and minor details. The Mother must be free, must be one and united, must have Her will supreme. Then it maybe that she gives out this Her will wearing a kingly crown on Her head or a republican gown round Her sacred form. Independence, Unity, and Parliament—this is the *mantra* which we will not sheath our sword till we see realised, not in its parts, as it would lead to the repetition of the past mistake and horrors, but and therefore, in its entirety and at once.

This, in short, is the line of action which is likely to be adopted by the Young Indians in evolving out the future of their nation.

The Fears and the Misgivings of the Indian Princes in relation to the present movement can be classified into two departments. For want of mutual understanding, the princes seem to be afraid of a revolution in the country on account of a possible recurrence of the past or innovation of the future. But for this fear, there is not a single man in the land who would not hail the independence of the Mother.

The Recurrence of the Past

The fear on the part of the princes of the recurrence of

the past owes its origin to the fear that is persistently made to hover around them by the cunning enemy, that "as soon as the strong hand of the British is removed from India the political balance will be upset and the Mahrattas and the Moghuls and the Sikhs will be fighting over the land once again." Granting for a moment that the revolution, after it has killed the hydra-headed foreign tyrant, would only end in setting up the past again, are you, we ask, O Princes, are you serious and in your senses, when you think of it as a reason to hug the present as the better state of the two? What, the times of Alab Singh, the founder of the Patiala state, are worse than this enervating death-peace in Patiala? The times when Guru Govind created the *Khalsa* are worse than the times when the *Khalsa* is a coolie and a slave? The times when your fathers could create these states and principalities are more to be feared than the present times when imbecility is trembling even to preserve those states? What, the time when the Scindia could march at the head of thousands, when Amritsar could be reared up, when Vikram could rule, when Kalidas could write, when the very Gods left heaven to have a bath in the Ganges or a Ras in the Vrindaven, are worse, say you, more to be hated, than these present times when none but Adversity can prosper, when none but Death can live?

Granting then that the revolution would end only in the recurrence of the past, none but an ignoramus in history can be afraid of it. We are not Negroes or Malays to be ashamed of our past! But glorious as it is, a thousand times more than the present, it is not the past that we would any longer strive to have. The past is glorious, but we want a future still more glorious. The light of the past has guided us so far, but we want to go further and want a brighter light. The Indian princes need not be afraid of the recurrence of the past, for we will not allow any one of them to encroach upon others, the existing rights and privileges of all of them will be strictly reflected and the provincial or individual bias will be made subservient to the all-powerful majesty of the Nation. The German people were exactly in the same position as we, and their solution of the problem is at once an example and a key to it, which would not fail to create confidence in the hearts of the princes of India. Once more we repeat that Independence, Unity, and Parliamentary rights of the people is our programme and banner, our faith and mission; and it excludes the recurrence of the past as decisively as the continuance of this hateful present.

The Innovation of the Future

This might be the second and perhaps a most potent fear than the first. But the ideal of state that we have already set before us disarms the potency of this second fear as effectively as it does that of the first. We cannot if we would and we would not if we could, try to sweep off the revered blood of the mighty spirits of our race, as if we do not feel the eternal gratitude due to the children of those who fought for us and died for us. For what are these Indian princes but so many glorious chapters of our national history, spread before us in letters of gold and diamond, in which, on one side, we read the bravery, the patriotism and the nobility of the flowers of our race and, on the other, the loyal recognition of their services by the grateful millions of our people? It is not the man that we see in Maharaja of Udaipur but it is the noble story of the immortal Pratap, how he fought and how he died for the pride of our land, for the honour of our race! The very jewels of their crowns, given as they are to their dynasties by a grateful nation are a sacred trust too national to be tarnished by petty spots. Mazzini was great and great were his principles; but the Indian princes need not be disturbed by his republican teachings as the Maharaja of Gwalior seems to be. No, the Indian princes need not be afraid of any republican innovation of the future which would undermine the loyalty of the Indian people to these ancient thrones, on account of the theoretical maxims of any republican prophet or statesman—be he even the great Italian himself.

Does not history bear us out? Do the princes think that even their present petty and subordinate existence would have been allowed to them by the foreign tyrant whose hunger ever grew on what is consumed, if the people had not risen to protect their right of adoption and to prevent the nefarious policy of confiscations in 1857? The people paid for your safety by shedding their blood and the very defeat of that immortal war of 1857 checked the greed of the tyrant, threatening him, from the grave, "Thus far and no further!" The men of *Abhinava Bharat* are not instigated by a destructive fury but are inspired by a constructive vision. From us, O Princes, expect nothing but light and liberty. As long as loyalty and patriotism coincide, as they have done all along the ancient history of India, so long there cannot be any antagonism between the people and their king. You have struck deep root in our soil. You are no mushroom growth. The stars in their courses have hedged you round with something like holiness and sanctity. Even your mistakes have been and will be forgiven unto seventy times and seven, and if you fall at all, it will not be owing to the destructive fury or mad republicanism of *Abhinava Bharat* but through your determination to commit political suicide.

The only innovation of the future, the only thing upon which we will insist is that the Indian princes should grant constitutions to their people and should recognise the unity of the nation and sovereignty of the Commonwealth, whether in a monarchical or republican form. Their position will be just like the position of the German princes. To recognise the sovereignty of their Mother, and that for their own benefit, is surely no terrible innovation for those to bear, who willingly or unwillingly are made to prostrate and sully their crowns at the feet of the lowborn *Mlechha*, at the wheels of whose chariots they are dragged from Calcutta to Simla and from Simla to Calcutta! By granting a constitution to their people and recognising the sovereignty of their Mother, the Indian princes would only regain the lustre of the past and gather strength for the future. For, are not the German princes better, stronger, for the unity and consolidation of their country? You have seen the Mikado; is he more powerful for having given his people the constitution, or less? Look at the *Sultan* of Turkey; is he more feared and honoured now by the world, or less? Look at King Edward of England; is he less prosperous and less firmly established, for allowing his people to guide him freely, than Charles I who was beheaded or James II who was driven from his throne? Think of this and step forward, the people guarantee you your hereditary thrones, crowns, and possessions, and would offer you seats in the Upper House of the National Assembly, where each of you would have power to vote and determine the destinies and laws of the Motherland. More loved at home and more honoured abroad, you would be respected and treated with all the reverence due to your exalted position by a people affectionate and great. This is all the innovation of the future! Advance, then, O Princes of India, boldly and bravely; there is nothing but your chains to lose!

Is She Not Your Mother Too?

Again, O Indian Princes, did not the land of *Bharat* give birth to you too? You too have sucked the mother's milk at Her breast. You too have breathed Her air. It was under Her trees that you experienced the first kiss of love. Her rivers cooled the parched-up lips of your mothers, Her moonlit nights the worried forehead of your father. Then, O Indian Princes, you too, like anyone of us, are bound by solemn bonds, to serve Her, to liberate Her—your ashes of your sires, the cradle of the first-born of your love! May further, Custodians of the honour of our race as you are, you ought to be the first to sacrifice yourselves, not because it is profitable but because it is your *Dharma*, because you who wear the crowns must fulfil the obligations of the crown. This is your *Raja-Dharma*—to serve the Mother as Pratap did, as Shivaji did. Never before was the glory of creating a nation of 300 million within the reach of the first man who but dares to stretch his arms! The people are waiting for a banner which would lead them to sacrifice and resurrection, and anyone who unfurls it on the battlefield of liberty will receive the ungrudging homage of grateful people. There is a crown, magnificent and matchless, compared with which the diadems of Ashoka and Vikram, of Akbar and Shivaji, are but fragments—crown anointed by the waters of the Ganges and set with the pearls of Ormuz and of Ind, in homage to which bend down the loftiest peaks of the Himalayas! Such a crown lies there in the hands of Mother Ind to be given as the prize for the first of Her royal born sons who would smite the foreign foe! Is there anyone amongst you, O ye Princes, who can but stretch his hand? Is there anyone amongst you who is ambitious enough to risk his coronet—tarnished and dirty on account of the slavery it covers—for the attainment of this glorious crown? to die indulging in the very dreams of whose lustre is far more honourable and pleasing than to live as caparisoned beasts to adorn the triumph of the alien foe? and beautiful enough to aspire to this goal not as a right but as a Dharma, for the good of the Mother and for the glory of God? If there be such a one, to his sceptre we bow—sceptre that drives the foreigners away and grants the constitution to the people!

But if there is none amongst you who can risk his all and offer his blood for the sake of the Mother, even then you can do well by at least not standing in the way of those who fight for the Mother. Never before was austere duty reduced to such easy inaction. The people will fight, the people will sacrifice their blood and the mother will be free without the least sacrifice on your part. All that you should do for us is to do nothing at all. Help us if not by cooperation, at least by inertia; if not by word at least by silence. Remembering the services of your ancestors, we will admit you to the share of the glory and the profit of the victory without asking you to contribute to its tremendous cost. Nothing can be easier than this, nothing can be more harmless than this!

A strict account will be asked of your doing and non-doings; and a people new-born will not fail to pay you in the coin that you paid. Every one of you who risks his own and joins us will get additions to his land, permanence to his family, and lustre to his name. Everyone who at least remains neutral and silent shall be confirmed in his estate and shall have the ordinary right to vote in the imperial chamber. But everyone who might have actively betrayed the trust of the people, disowned his fathers, and debased his blood, by arraying himself against the Mother—he shall be crushed to dust and ashes, and shall be looked upon as a helot, a bastard, and a renegade. His estate shall be confiscated and distributed amongst the faithful princes, and he shall be hurled down with curse of the whole nation to the doom of the traitor's death! Take our word seriously, for it is likely that you would be deduced still further, as the force of this infant revolution, being spiritual, are too subtle to be grasped by the ordinary sight, and the power of the foreign tyrant, being material and therefore palpable, looks gigantic to be overthrown. "Every new idea is at the beginning in the minority of precisely one." Christianity was so when the Caesar who wanted to crush it was the mightiest on earth. But look now! The Roman Emperor is a myth of the past, while that Christianity has conquered "regions which Caesars never knew." It is His wish who created the *Himalayas* on our north and Ceylon on our south that India shall be one, shall be free, shall be a nation. *Abhinava Bharat* has heard His word, has seen His vision, has received His command to do and die—to die and do. Do you doubt our grim earnestness? If so, hear the name of Dhingra and be dumb! In the name of that Martyr, O Indian Princes, we ask you to think solemnly and deeply upon these words and choose your path. Choose what you will, and you will reap what you sow. Choose whether you should be the first of the nation's Fathers or the last of the nation's tyrants!

Vande Matram

❑

Two Poems of Savarkar

The Revolutionist to Himself

From out the Chinese prison was set free
He, who for twenty years no light could see
So! He implores the guards with weeping yell
"Pray take me back to my old happy cell."
"Happier to you is dungeon than this light?"
"This Sun divine worse than the endless night!"
"Ah! yells the captive 'light I cannot bear!'
My chains me spare the troubles of freedom's care!!"
Alas! my nation through the slothful ease
Like this wretch dreads the freedom's lusty breeze.
Accustomed grown to the life of living death,
It hates life living and its active breath!
They love the shackles and hate its breaking, lest
The noise of hammering might disturb their rest!
Fear me too—if hate not! –me, who to free
Them from dreadful den of shame, as fee
Have coined my heart's fresh blood and having killed
The self in me in youth grew old and chilled
Homeless I, so that they might get back Home
That they might rest an exile I do roam
That they may mount throne, I mount the scaffolds bold.
Thorny crown I wear, that they might wear of gold!
Yet me they hate for having loved them well
Advise me to fall as meanly as they fell!
They touch not me but shake hands with the foe

Me they walk not with but with dastards go
But stop ye thoughts! Illumine, me, uphold
Thy healing charms of Duty do unfold!
The dust of Present let not dim my sight
Unto the vision future's; let not might
Unnerve the dawn of hope! It must be so
That none shall pity thee, nor mercy show
Alone, deserted, sad, must wander thou
In search of Dharma the lost treasure now
That when revealed, the world might worship thee
As relic proud thy hair would beg on kneel
Avoid they shall to go with you today
But millions will thy trumpet call obey!
Prahlad and Buddha and Mazzini show
Fanatics all they first who prophets grow!
Let polar star of Dharma sole be thy guide
Success, defeat, nor flame, nor praise, nor pride,
What if return they, curses for my love
The surgeon's hand diseased hate all above
Hate they me for regenerations toil
Greater the reason then why I my soil
Should serve the more! Work for them I will
In spite of all their faults I love them still
God Almighty pray I this to you.
"Forgive them Lord! They know not what they do."
One race, one blood, one flesh! All children we
Upon one fondling breath has nursed us She
Our glorious mother! her pride let us guard
Her service sweet! it is its own reward!!

(London 1909)

The Farewell

Whose heart-to-heart by silken ties is knit
Of friendship sweet, that sweeter grow by far,
Partaking of Godly Sacrament of Mother's creed divine:
Oh friends! Farewell! as tender and fresh
As the morning dew that wakes the fragrance
Friends adieu! adieu!

God-appointed Duty

We part to play our God-appointed parts
Now pent and nailed to burning Rocks, now tossed
On surging waves of fame; now seen now lost
Or humble or exalted—wherever posted by the Lord
Of Hosts, yet posted best, as if alone it was
The mission of our life thus there to act.

Historic Stage

As in some oriental play sublime,
All characters, the dead as well as living
In Epilogue they meet
Thus actors we innumerable all once more shall meet
On History's copious stage before the great
Applauding audience of Humanity
That would with grateful cheer fill hill and dale
Till then, Oh loving friends, Farewell!! Farewell!!

Humanity to Guide

Wherever may my humble ashes lie
In the Andamans' sad brook whose weeping course
Add to its dreariness a tongue or stored by Ganga's
Sacred crystal stream in which the stars
Their midnight measures dance—
They will be stirred with fire and glow
When Victory's trumpet, blasts proclaiming
"Shree Ram" has crowned his chosen people's brow
With laurels golden green! The evil spirit is cast
Away and chased back to the deep from whence

It first arose! And Lo! She lordly stands,
Our Mother Ind, a beacon light Humanity to guide,
Oh martyred saints and soldiers, do awake!
The battle is won which you fought and fell!!
Till then, Oh loving friends, Farewell!! Farewell!!

Sacrifice a Law

Watch sleeplessly the progress of our mother
And learn to count it, not by so much work
Done or tried, but by how much they suffered
What sacrifice our people could sustain!
For work is chance but sacrifice a law;
Foundation firm to rear a mighty Dome
Of Kingdoms new and great!
But only great if their roots be in martyr's ashes laid
Thus work for Mother's glory till God's breath
Be rendered back, the Godly mission done—
A martyr's wreath or victor's crown be won!!

❑

Echoes from the Andamans

Excerpts from the epistles that Savarkar wrote from his solitary cell in Port Blair to his family

Those who work outside work much; but those who work in the prison work more. Suffering is itself work—intense but subtle.

***

At bottom, work, if true, is suffering; and suffering, if true, is work. Suffering is the motor, the power that moves, and goads and propels a people. Unless the best amongst us suffer, the rest cannot work.

***

'We will work and die in defence of Righteousness'—thus had we pledged our words. Behold! We enter the flames! We have kept our words.

***

It was on this altar that I sacrificed my health and my wealth. Neither the longing looks of my young wife vainly waiting for my return nor the peals of laughter of dear children, nor the helplessness of a sister-in-law would hold me back at the call of thy trumpet.

***

I believe in a universal state embracing all mankind and wherein all men and women would be citizens working for and enjoying equally the fruits of this earth and this Sun, this land and this light which constitute the real Motherland and Fatherland of man. All other divisions and distinctions are artificial though indispensable.

Political prisoners means all those undergoing imprisonment whether convicted or not, whether for individual acts or acts in general (I indeed fail to understand it altogether) for actions which proceeded from purely and admittedly political motives. The term 'political' can be distinguished from private only by the criterion of the motive of that act itself. No act is or can be by itself political. For even a rebellion, for that proceeds entirely for my own bread and butter, is not political and ought not to create any sympathy in others.

***

A revolution is evolution in leaps. We are revolutionaries under necessity and not by choice. Even while combating force with force we heartily abhorred and do ye abhor all violence. For violence is force aggressively used—force that is life-killing.

***

I saw it used by powerful combinations against their weaker, but righteous rivals. I have always abhorred violence of ambitious men and nations not only outside India but even in India herself. I felt as rebellious against the caste system and the untouchability inside India as her being dominated by foreigners from outside.

***

Jails (such as the Andamans) have a great sustaining power. They corrode but they do not kill. They petrify; but they preserve.

***

Ready I am who found the honey of life sweet, whose eyes enjoyed the light and whose heart thrilled at the touch of love.

***

Ready I am to bear even the agonies of death ungrudgingly as a price which one is bound in duty to pay for having loved these blessings of life.

***

After having sparkled brilliantly a while like a pleasant rainbow in the sky of consciousness if this 'I' of me is swiftly dissolved and disappears into the universal 'I' that is inlaid in Nature—then, O' Death—death thou art but deliverance.

❑

Bibliography

Primary Sources:

Works by V D Savarkar

My Transportation for Life, translation of *Majhi Janmathep*, by V N Naik, 2nd Edition. Bombay: Veer Savarkar Prakashn, 1984.

Biographies

Kranti Ke Naksastra. Trans. Ramesh Gupta, and ed. Bhagirath Pravasi. New Delhi: Rajdhani Granthagar, 1982.

Mazzini. 2nd Edition. Pune: Venus Prakashan, 1946.

Dramas

Pratisodh, translation of *Uttarkriya*. Trans. Vikram Singh. New Delhi: Bhartiya Sahitya Sadan, 1969.

Sastra Aur Saastra, translation of *Sanyast Khadga*. Trans. Vikram Singh. New Delhi: Rajdhani Granthagar, 1968.

Usap. Trans. Vikram Singh. New Delhi: Rajdhani Granthagar, 1977.

Essays

Bhasha Suddhi. 2nd edition. Bombay: Maharasthra Rajya Sahitya Publication, 1981.

Hamari Samasyaen. Delhi: Rajpal and Sons. N.D.

Hindu Rastravad. Ed. Satya Prakash. Rohtak: Satya Prakash, 1945.

Hindu Dhawaja. Bombay: Veer Savarkar Prakashan, 1985.

Hinduva Ke Panch Pran. Trans. Vikram Singh. New Delhi: Bharti Publication, 1979.

Kranti Ghos. Ed. Balarao Savarkar. Bombay: Divine Publication, 1979.

Savarkar Vichar Darshan. Trans. C B Kelkar and Ed. Bhanu Pratap Shukla. Lucknow: Lok Hita Prakashan, 1970.

Fiction

Gomantak. Trans. Madhavraj Mule. 3rd Edition. New Delhi: Bharti Sahitya Sadan, 1983.

Kala Pani. New Delhi: Bharti Sahitya Sadan, 1983.

Mopla. New Delhi: Rajdhani Granthagar, 1981.

History

Hindu Pad-Padasuahi. 6th Edition. New Delhi: Rajdhani Granthagar, 1961.

Hindu Rastravad. Ed. Satya Prakash. Rohtak: Satya Prakash, 1945.

Indian War of Independence. 8th Edition. New Delhi: Rajdhani Granthagar, 1985.

Poetry

Kamala. Trans. B L Ranaday. Bombay: B L Ranaday, 1979.

Mahasagar. Trans. B L Ranaday. Bombay: Veer Savarkar Prakashan, 1986.

Saptarishi. Trans. B L Ranaday. Bombay: B L Ranaday, 1971.

Virahocchavas. Trans. B L Ranaday. Bombay: Savarkar Prakashan, 1986.

Collected Works

Samagra Savarkar Vangmaya, Vols 1-8. Pune: Samagra Savarkar Vangmaya Prakashan Samiti, 1963.

Secondary Sources: Biographical and Critical Studies

Abbots, J S C. *Life of Napoleon Bonaparte*. New Delhi: Kalyani Publishers, 1972.

Aldred, Guy. *No Traitor's Gait*. Glasgow: The Strickland Press, 1956.

---------------. "Gandhi, Pacifism, and India," *The World Quarterly*, Vol I, No 1 (Spring 1950): 4-7.

Anand, V S. *Savarkar: A Study in the Evolution of Indian Nationalism*. London: Woolf, 1967.

Aphle, Govindswami. *Savarkar Gaatha*. Pune: Govindswami Aphle, 1967.

Atre, Prahlad Keshav. *Savarkar Sahitya Navneet*. Bombay: Maharasthra Granth Bhandar, 1958.

Banerjee, S N. *A Nation in Making*. Madras: Oxford University Press, 1925.

Bhave, P B. *Savarkar Navachi Jyoti*. Pune: Sun Publications, 1983.

Brown, E C. *Har Dayal: Hindu Revolutionary and Rationalist*. New Delhi: Manohar Book Services, 1975.

Chirol, Valentine. *Indian Unrest*. Revised and Enlarged from the Times London. London: Macmillan, 1910.

Choudhari, K K. *Maharashtra and Indian Freedom Struggle*. Bombay: Govt. of Maharashtra Information and Public Relations, 1985.

Coxe, Williams. *La Empereur Napolean*. London: Longmans, 1819.

Datta, V N. *Madanlal Dhingra and the Revolutionary Movement*. New Delhi: Vikas Publications House, 1978.

Dharamveer. *Bhai Parmanand Aur Unka Yug*. Delhi: Bhai Parmanand Samarak Samiti, 1981.

Elst, Koenraad. *Gandhi and Godse*, Rev Edition. New Delhi: Voice of India, 2012.

Gharpure, K V. *Swatantraveer Savarkar: Vyakti Aur Tatavajnan*. Nagpur: Savarkar Tatvajnana Prasar Kendra, 1967.

Gandhi, Tushar A. *Let us kill Gandhi: A Chronicle of His Last Days, the Conspiracy, Murder, Investigation and Trial*, New Delhi: Rupa and Co, 2007.

Garnett, David. *The Golden Echo, Vol I*. London: Chatto & Windus, 1970.

Gawade, P L. *Vinayak Damodar Savarkar: Ek Chikitsak Abhyas*. Pune: Swadhayaya Mahavidhyalaya Prakashan, 1970.

Ghosh, Tapan. *Gandhi Murder Case*. Delhi: Asia Publication House, 1974.

Godse, Gopal. *Jaya Mritunjaya, 2nd Edition*. Pune: Vitasta Prakashan, 1979.

Godse, Nathuram. *May It Please Your Honour*. Delhi: Surya Bharati Prakashan, 2007.

Goel, Shiv Kumar. *Amar Senani Savarkar: Jeevan Jhanki*. New Delhi: Bharti Sahitya Sadan, 1983.

--------------------. *Vinayak Damodar Savarkar: Jeevan aur Darshan*. New Delhi: Bharti Sahitya Sadan, N.D.

Gupta, Chitra. *Life of Barrister Savarkar*. Madras: B G Paul & Co, 1926.

Gupta, Chitra and Indra Prakash. *Life of Barrister Savarkar*. Lahore: Hindu Mission Press, 1939.

Gupta, Manmathnath. *Bharat ke Krantikari*. Delhi: Hind Pocket Books, 1969.

---------------------. *History of the Indian Revolutionary Movement*. Bombay: Somaiya Publications, 1972.

Hardas, Balashstri. *Armed Struggle for Freedom: Ninety Years War of Indian Independence, 1857-1947.* Trans S SApte. Poona: S R Date, 1958.

Joshi, G M. *Death Conqueror: Veer Savarkar*. Ed. Balarao Savarkar. Bombay: Veer Savarkar Prakashan, 1976.

Kakatkar, N V. *Bhartiya Swatantrata ka Itihas*, 2 Volumes. Lucknow: Rashtradharam Pustak Prakashan, 1968.

Kallol, A. *Swatantrayaveer Savarkar*. Trans Padmakar Bhare. Nagpur: Bharat Bharti, 1980.

Keer, Dhananjaya. *Veer Savarkar*. Pune: Asmita Prakashan, 1966.

Kelkar, B K. *Samaj Sudharak Savarkar*. Pune: Asmita Prakashan, 1986.

Khadikar, Madhav. *Swantrayaveer Savarkar Yanchaya Tejasvi Jeevan Gatha*. Pune: Tridal Prakashan, 1985.

Khole, Vilas, Ed. *Suryabimaca Sodh*. Pune: Shodh Prakashan, N.D.

Majumdar, R C., Gen Ed. *Struggle for Freedom*. Bombay: Bhartiya Vidya Bhavan, 1969.

Malgonkar, Manohar. *The Men who Killed Gandhi*. New Delhi: Roli Books, 2008.

Marathe, Govindrao. *Vinayak Damodar Savarkar*. Prayag: Chhatra Hitkari Pustakamala, 1947.

Murthy, M S N. *Madame Cama*. Bangalore: Rashtrothan Sahiyta, 1973.

Oak, V G. *Hindu Maha Sabha Neeti Darshan*. New Delhi: Akhil Bharat Hindu Mahasabha, 1982.

Padmanabhan, R A. *V V S Aiyar*. New Delhi: National Book Trust, 1980.

Ridley, Jasper. *Garibaldi*. New York, Viking Press, 1976.

Salvi, A G. *Swatantrayaveer Savarkaranchaya Sahvasant, 2nd Edition*, 2 Volumes. Ratnagiri: A G Salvi, 1976.

Savarkar, Balarao. *Veer Savarkar and Gandhi ji*. Bombay: Veer Savarkar Prakashan, 1969.

--------------------. *Mahayogi Veer Savarkar*. Bombay: Veer Savarkar Prakashan, 1969.

--------------------. *Swatantraya Veer Savarkar Darsan*. Bombay: Veer Savarkar Prakashan, 1983.

--------------------. *Swatantraya Veer Savarkar*: Ratnagiri Parv, Vol 1, Bombay: Veer Savarkar Prakashan, 1973.

--------------------. *Swatantraya Veer Savarkar: Hindu Mahasabha Parv*, Vol 2. Bombay: Veer Savarkar Prakashan, 1975.

--------------------. *Swatantraya Veer Savarkar: Akhand Hindustan Lada Parv*. Bombay: Veer Savarkar Prakashan, 1976.

--------------------. *Swatantraya Veer Savarkar: Saangta Parv*. Bombay: Veer Savarkar Prakashan, 1986.

Shastri, Premchand. *Swatantraya Veer Savarkar*: *Jeevan Darsan*. New Delhi: Arya Prakashan, 1981.

Singhal, M G. *Swantrataya Veer Savarkar*. Meerut: Gopal Printing Press, N. D.

Singh, Banarasi. *London mein Goli*. New Delhi: Rajdhani Granthagar, 1977.

-------------------. *Punya Smaran: Mritunjaya Savarkar*. New Delhi: Akhil Bharat Hindu Mahasabha, 1966.

Sinha, B K. *In Andamans: The Indian Bastille*. Kanpur: Profulla C Mitra, 1939.

Sonpati, Mukund. *Darya Par*. Pune: Purendare Prakashan, 1980.

Srivastava, Harindra. *Five Stormy Years: Savarkar in London*. New Delhi: Allied Publishers, 1983.

------------------------*Savarkar London mein: Paanch Toofani Varsh. Delhi:* Rajpal Sons, 1984.

The World Quarterly, Special Double Number on Gandhi Murder Trial, Vol I, No 1 (Spring 1950). Glasgow: The Strickland Press, 1950.

Vidyalankar, Vijay. *Veer Savarkar*. Delhi: Shiksha Bharti, 1984.

Vyas, V D. *Swatantraya Veer Vinayak Damodar Savarkaranchaya Jeevanavar Khand Kavya*. Solapore: V D Vyas, 1983.

Yajnik, I L. *Shyamji Krishnavarma: Life and Times of an Indian Revolutionary*. Bombay: Lakshmi Publication, 1950.

❑

The British Museum Library where Savarkar wrote his revoluntionary book 'The Indian War of Independence'. The book was instantly banned by the British Parliament even before the publication of its first chapter —something unprecedented in the history of the world.

प्रधान मन्त्री भारत

PRIME MINISTER,
INDIA

No.836-PMO/80

New Delhi,
May 20, 1980

Dear Shri Bakhle,

I have received your letter of the 8th May 1980.

Veer Savarkar's daring defiance of the British Government has its own important place in the annals of our freedom movement. I wish success to the plans to celebrate the birth centenary of this remarkable son of India.

Yours sincerely,

Indira Gandhi

(Indira Gandhi)

Shri Pandit Bakhle,
Secretary,
Swatantrayaveer Savarkar
Rashtriya Smarak,
252, Swatantrayaveer Savarkar Marg,
Shivaji Park, Dadar, Bombay - 40002

PRIME MINISTER

MESSAGE

It is heartening to note that the Swatantryaveer Savarkar Rashtriya Smarak, Bombay is bringing out a special Commemorative volume on the occasion of Veer Savarkar's 110th Birth Anniversary on May 28, 1993. Veer Savarkar was a great patriot who imparted a revolutionary fervour to our freedom movement. His writings reveal an abiding commitment to social reform. Such constructive chanelling of the energies of the youth is what our nation needs today for strength and prosperity.

I hope that the articles in this Commemorative volume will bring about a better understanding of Veer Savarkar's philosophy.

New Delhi
December 18, 1992

[P.V. Narasimha Rao]

Standing on either side of the flag designed by Savarkar and hoisted by Madam Cama in Stuttgart is the author & his wife Ravi Srivastava,
The flag is safely preserved by S.S. Rana's grandson Shri Rajendra Singh Rana, MP

वीर सावरकर द्वारा निर्मित

हिन्दू राष्ट्र ध्वज

सूरत हिन्दू महासभा अधिवेशन (1929)

इदं मे ब्रह्म च क्षत्रं श्रियमश्नुताम्।

(यजुर्वेद)

धर्म का ज्ञान (विचारधारा) और धर्म का क्षेत्र (राजनीति) दोनों
श्री (विजय और वैभव) प्रदान करते हैं।

हिन्दू अपने हिन्दू राष्ट्र ध्वज के महत्व को समझें और संगठित एवं तेजस्वी हों।

❑❑❑